TECHNICAL
REPORT

# Qatar Supreme Council for Family Affairs Database of Social Indicators

## Final Report

Lynn A. Karoly, Michael Mattock

Prepared for the Qatar Supreme Council for Family Affairs

 RAND-QATAR POLICY INSTITUTE

This research was sponsored by the Qatar Supreme Council for Family Affairs and conducted within RAND Labor and Population and the RAND-Qatar Policy Institute, programs of the RAND Corporation.

**Library of Congress Cataloging-in-Publication Data**

Karoly, Lynn A., 1961–
    Qatar Supreme Council for Family Affairs : database of social indicators : final report / Lynn A. Karoly, Michael Mattock.
        p. cm. — (TR ; 350)
    Includes bibliographical references.
    ISBN 0-8330-3947-4 (pbk.)
    1. Family—Qatar. 2. Family policy—Qatar. 3. Social indicators—Qatar. 4. Qatar. Majlis al-
A'lá li-Shu'ūn al-Usrah. I. Mattock, Michael G., 1961–  . II. Title. III. Series: Technical report (Rand Corporation) ; 350.

HQ665.7.K37 2006
306.85095363—dc22

                2006011005

The RAND Corporation is a nonprofit research organization providing objective analysis and effective solutions that address the challenges facing the public and private sectors around the world. RAND's publications do not necessarily reflect the opinions of its research clients and sponsors.

**RAND®** is a registered trademark.

© Copyright 2006 RAND Corporation

All rights reserved. No part of this book may be reproduced in any form by any electronic or mechanical means (including photocopying, recording, or information storage and retrieval) without permission in writing from RAND.

Published 2006 by the RAND Corporation
1776 Main Street, P.O. Box 2138, Santa Monica, CA 90407-2138
1200 South Hayes Street, Arlington, VA 22202-5050
4570 Fifth Avenue, Suite 600, Pittsburgh, PA 15213
RAND URL: http://www.rand.org/
To order RAND documents or to obtain additional information, contact
Distribution Services: Telephone: (310) 451-7002;
Fax: (310) 451-6915; Email: order@rand.org

# Preface

The Qatar Supreme Council for Family Affairs (QSCFA) is developing a social indicators database system. The database will help monitor the well-being of families in Qatar and provide information for future planning and decisionmaking within the six domains of the QSCFA: the family, women, children, youth, the elderly, and people with special needs. The RAND-Qatar Policy Institute (RQPI) is under contract with the QSCFA to assist in planning for and developing the database. This document serves as the final report for the project. In addition to the sponsor, the report may be of interest to other governmental institutions in Qatar that interact with the QSCFA, as well as similar institutions in other countries considering the development of such a database system.

This research was sponsored by the Qatar Supreme Council for Family Affairs and conducted within RAND Labor and Population and the RAND-Qatar Policy Institute, programs of the RAND Corporation.

The opinions expressed and conclusions drawn in this report are the responsibility of the authors and do not represent the official views of the QSCFA, other agencies, the RAND Corporation, or RQPI.

# Contents

# Figures

# Tables

# Summary

The Qatar Supreme Council for Family Affairs, established in 1998 under the authority of His Highness the Emir, is charged with reviewing and proposing legislation, promoting policies, adopting plans, implementing projects and programs, enhancing the role of national institutions, and disseminating information related to all aspects of family affairs in Qatar. The mission is defined through nine goals pertaining to the role and care of families, the challenges facing families, the goals of international charters relating to family matters, the empowerment and participation of women in society and in the labor market, the status of people with special needs, and the challenges facing youth. Six operating departments carry out these goals, each focusing on a specific population in Qatar: the family, women, children, youth, the elderly, and people with special needs

In support of its mission, the Qatar Supreme Council for Family Affairs is developing a social indicators database system. The database will provide essential information for assessing the well-being of families in Qatar, planning future activities, monitoring progress toward departmental goals, and setting policy priorities. A centralized database will provide an efficient mechanism for supporting the activities of the QSCFA and will assist in coordinating work across departments with overlapping interests.

This document provides the final results of an analysis in support of this database effort by the RAND-Qatar Policy Institute. In this report, we focus in particular on the following questions:

- What are the goals of the database system and how do they relate to the objectives of the QSCFA?

- What indicators are best suited to supporting the goals of the database system and how should they be measured?

- Are data available to compute the indicators?

- What architecture will best support the database system?

To address these questions, we undertook a review of the QSCFA's goals and the current mission and potential future activities of the QSCFA departments, studied the architecture and indicators included in the prototype database, and reviewed the major available sources of data to construct most of the indicators of interest. This summary highlights key recommendations distributed throughout the chapters of this report. All recommendations featured here are summarized in Table S.1.

## Database Objectives

The content and objectives of the QSCFA database can be viewed in terms of both short-term and long-term benefits with regard to the work of the Council as summarized in Figure S.1. The most immediate goal is to create a database of summary indicators that will support the analysis, planning, and decisionmaking of the QSCFA and its various departments. For example, the database of summary indicators may be used to

- track progress over time in a given domain for a given outcome,

- compare alternative measures of a given indicator,

- examine indicators for population subgroups or geographic areas, and

- generate statistics for QSCFA reports or for international agency reports.

In the short-term, most indicators stored in the database will be generated from data collected by other agencies in the Qatari public sector, such as the Planning Council or other government departments.

Over the longer-term, the database content and objectives may be expanded in order to provide even greater support of analysis, planning, and decisionmaking. Beyond monitoring trends or identifying gaps between current achievement and targets, there may be an interest in determining the causes of the observed trends or gaps in progress, identifying subpopulations that are particularly affected, and formulating and evaluating policy interventions. Those objectives will require analytic tools and data that go beyond what a database of summary indicators can provide.

In particular, we anticipate two future directions for the QSCFA in terms of data generation, manipulation, and consumption.

Table S.1—Summary of Recommendations

---

**Recommendations**

---

Regarding the database objectives:
- ¬  Develop the social indicators database system with both short-term and long-term goals in mind.

Regarding the social indicators database content:
- ¬  Build a social indicators database system flexible enough to accommodate multiple indicators, store indicators for multiple years, allow indicators to be analyzed as levels or rates, record indicators in aggregate or for disaggregated groups or geographic areas, and add new fields for each indicator over time or add new indicators over time.

- ¬  Cover the following broad domains in the social indicators database system: population, economy, family life, education, health and nutrition, environment, civil and political life, safety and security, and statutes.

- ¬  Include, for the various individual indicators, a number of specific fields relevant to that indicator.

Regarding the social indicators database indicators:
- ¬  Populate the database based on a detailed list of 373 indicators.

- ¬  Prioritize the list of indicators to allocate resources effectively.

Regarding refining the list of indicators:
- ¬  Reevaluate the set of indicators on at least an annual basis.

- ¬  For indicators that are discontinued, determine the treatment of information stored in the database.

- ¬  For indicators that are added to the database, determine whether historical information will be stored along with contemporary and future data.

- ¬  Review the database fields to determine whether new fields are needed, or whether old ones can be discontinued.

- ¬  Communicate to users on a regular basis changes in the database indicators and fields.

Regarding the measurement of database indicators generally:
- ¬  Carefully determine the underlying population for any given indicator so that comparisons over time are consistent.

- ¬  Record indicators in the database, where relevant and feasible, as both levels and rates.

- ¬  Obtain, where possible and relevant, estimates of the standard errors associated with particular indicators.

Table S.1—Summary of Recommendations, Continued

---

**Recommendations**

---

Regarding the database architecture:

- ¬ Establish standards for electronic data exchange.

- ¬ Use a dedicated database management system (DBMS) for storage, manipulation, and retrieval of data.

- ¬ Adopt a three-tiered client/server database architecture: client, application server or Web server, and database server.

- ¬ Implement the user interface of the database as a Web browser application using non-proprietary standards, rather than a Lotus® Notes®/Domino®–specific application.

- ¬ Add a provision for ad hoc queries.

- ¬ Where appropriate, store the international standard classification numbers or codes used to refer to a particular indicator in a searchable field of the database.

Regarding strategic actions for future implementation of the social indicators database system:

- ¬ Develop a solid understanding of the various sources of data, their sample coverage, measures available, and strengths and limitations.

- ¬ Conduct a complete review of data gaps for the preferred list of indicators.

- ¬ Identify other indicators to examine in an in-depth review of measurements, data sources, and data quality.

- ¬ Determine whether some indicators must be recomputed to be consistent over time.

- ¬ Determine whether new data collection is required.

- ¬ Establish a formal mechanism for cooperation with the Planning Council in the implementation of the recommended database architecture.

Regarding longer-term objectives (microdata and data collection):

- ¬ Pursue development of a database with detailed information on individuals or families and the physical and human capacity to analyze such data.

---

- • *The QSCFA would benefit from having access to the underlying data used to generate the summary indicators.* These underlying data or "microdata" may include census or survey data, vital statistics data, or administrative data. Access to these detailed data will allow QSCFA staff to analyze the relationships between indicators, including cause-and-effect relationships, as well as to conduct studies of the relationships between specific policies and the outcomes they are designed to influence.

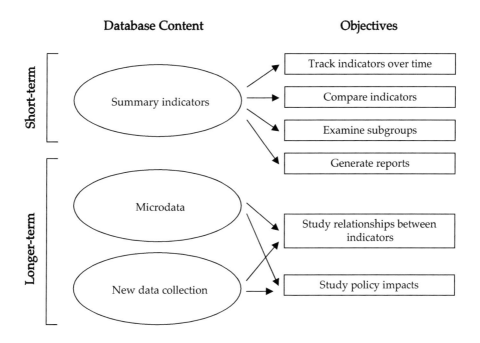

Figure S.1—Relationship Between Database Content and Objectives in the
Short-Term and Longer-Term

- *The QSCFA may become a producer of data.* Given the diverse program
  areas covered by the QSCFA and the associated unique data needs, new
  data collection may be required in support of policymaking at the
  Council. In some cases, the information needed by the Council may not
  be collected currently, or it may not be collected in the way needed to
  support the desired analyses. For example, there may be a need for
  special-purpose surveys that allow analyses of the relationships between
  multiple domains of family life (e.g., demographic, economic, health) or
  that allow analyses of the dynamics of family life through longitudinal
  information. Such multipurpose, longitudinal data are often collected
  through smaller, more intensive surveys, compared with larger-scale
  censuses or single-purpose cross-sectional surveys (e.g., labor force
  surveys, or health surveys).

¬ *Recommendation: Develop the social indicators database system with both
short-term and long-term goals in mind.*

Although the initial focus is on developing a comprehensive, reliable, and
accessible database of summary indicators, future developments should move in
the direction of developing the capacity for a database that can be used for wider

policy analysis. Ideally, decisions made in support of the short-term objectives will be consistent with the longer-term goals. Choices in the near-term that might hinder the longer-term objectives should be considered carefully to determine whether other options are available to support both sets of objectives.

In the remainder of the summary, we focus on the recommendations that follow from our in-depth analysis of the content, indicators, architecture, and data processing associated with the social indicators database system. These aspects are all relevant for meeting the short-term objectives of the QSCFA and its departments. Our recommendations regarding the short-term objectives also include several that pertain to the necessary strategic next steps for the QSCFA to meet the short-term database goals. We also highlight several recommendations that relate to the longer-term objectives, which may be considered in more depth in a future project.

## Short-Term Focus: Recommendations Regarding the Social Indicators Database System

In considering the requirements for the immediate objective of developing a social indicators database system, we focused on the database content, the indicators and their potential data sources, and the required architecture and data processing. The following section highlights our recommendations in each of these areas. We also feature several strategic recommendations associated with implementing the database.

### Database Content

Our analysis of database content leads to three recommendations pertaining to the database features, the domains covered by the data, and the key data elements. These recommendations build on the capabilities demonstrated by the current prototype database.

¬ *Recommendation: Build a social indicators database system flexible enough to accommodate multiple indicators, store indicators for multiple years, allow indicators to be analyzed as levels or rates, record indicators in aggregate or for disaggregated groups or geographic areas, and add new fields for each indicator over time or add new indicators over time.*

These features are consistent with the short-term objectives of the database, namely the ability to examine changes in indicators over time, compare alternative measures of the same indicator, examine population subgroups, and generate reports. The final feature ensures that the database can be modified over time to meet the evolving needs of the Council.

¬ *Recommendation: Cover the following broad domains in the social indicators database system: population, economy, family life, education, health and nutrition, environment, civil and political life, safety and security, and statutes.*

Given the breadth and depth of the issues facing the QSCFA departments and QSCFA staff who will use the database system, the subjects covered by the database should be equally comprehensive. Within each of the broad domains, detailed indicators will provide the information required for one or more QSCFA departments.

¬ *Recommendation: Include, for the various individual indicators, a number of specific fields relevant to that indicator.*

The specific fields we identified (some of which may involve more than one data element) include:

- Indicator label and definition

- Population unit

- Date of measurement

- Unit of measure

- Source of data

- Methodological notes

- Other fields to record additional key information.

## Database Indicators

The indicators in the database should be shaped by the needs of the primary database consumers, namely the staff in the six main departments of the Council, as well as the associated committees. Given their current mission and potential future goals, the Departments of Family and Women have perhaps the most wide-ranging data needs, covering a broad set of indicators and a variety of population subgroups. The Departments of Childhood, Youth, Elderly, and Special Needs have somewhat more specialized interests, at least in terms of well-defined population subgroups, although the subject areas of interest are equally broad.

Given the wide array of indicators that are of potential interest for the social indicators database system, there are a number of data sources from which these indicators can be drawn. These sources include national accounts, vital statistics, registries, administrative records, population and housing censuses, and other population-based surveys (e.g., Labor Force Survey, Household Expenditure and Income Survey, and Family Health Survey). In some cases, these data sources can provide data on a regular periodicity (e.g., monthly or annually), while other sources may be less frequent or even irregular (e.g., those based on periodic surveys).

Our assessment of the indicators for the database leads to two overarching recommendations; both involve very detailed information, provided in the body of the report.

¬ *Recommendation: Populate the database based on a detailed list of 373 indicators.*

We have provided a detailed list of indicators recommended for inclusion in the database. For each indicator, we have provided a definition and unit of measurement, referenced possible data sources, listed relevant population subgroups, and indicated the relevant departments and QSCFA goals. This list reflects indicators currently included in the prototype database, as well as other indicators recommended by the QSCFA departments and research staff as relevant to their objectives. We have also added other indicators that we believe are important for meeting the goals of the QSCFA and its departments.

¬ *Recommendation: Prioritize the list of indicators to allocate resources effectively.*

Given how extensive the list of indicators is, assigning a priority ranking will allow the QSCFA to assign resources by the importance of the indicators to the needs of the various departments and the ease with which the data can be obtained. We have provided our recommended rankings for each indicator based on a four-point scale. The QSCFA may wish to modify these rankings based on its own assessment of the relative priorities across indicators and the ease of obtaining the necessary data.

The list of indicators presented in this report should not be viewed as static. Indeed, there is an expectation that new indicators we have not covered will be needed in the future, while indicators currently recommended may no longer be required. For example, in the future, the QSCFA's mission may expand, new sources of data may become available, or new reporting requirements may be implemented. Thus, we also made several recommendations regarding the process for refining the list of indicators over time. In particular, five recommendations pertain to this issue:

- ¬ *Recommendation: Reevaluate the set of indicators on at least an annual basis.*

- ¬ *Recommendation: For indicators that are discontinued, determine the treatment of information stored in the database.*

- ¬ *Recommendation: For indicators that are added to the database, determine whether historical information will be stored along with contemporary and future data.*

- ¬ *Recommendation: Review the database fields to determine whether new fields are needed, or whether old ones can be discontinued.*

- ¬ *Recommendation: Communicate to users on a regular basis changes in the database indicators and fields.*

Most of these recommendations are self-explanatory. The purpose of the periodic review is to ensure that the indicators and database fields actively maintained in the database will be required to meet the current and future needs of the QSCFA and its departments and to determine whether there are any gaps in the indicators or fields. As indicators or fields are discontinued or added, decisions should be made regarding information already in the database (for the former), and the inclusion of historical data (for the latter). This process of annual review should be undertaken formally as part of a designated committee of QSCFA staff, with representation from the various functional and support departments. Changes should be communicated routinely to the user community, e.g., in writing or through a "bulletin board" accessible to users as part of the database interface.

Although this project was not designed to allow an in-depth analysis of the full set of recommended indicators, we did identify several measurement issues that are relevant for most of the recommended indicators. In this regard, we highlight three general recommendations regarding the measurement of database indicators.

- ¬ *Recommendation: Carefully determine the underlying population for any given indicator so that comparisons over time are consistent.*

Indicators that are population-based are measured for well-defined population groups or subgroups. Thus, it is crucial for the social indicators database system to provide a clear indication of the relevant population for each indicator, especially to facilitate comparisons of an indicator over time. For example, is the indicator measured for Qataris, non-Qataris, or both? Was the indicator calculated for people of all ages or only for those in a given age range? Was the indicator calculated only for those who met certain criteria (e.g., those who sought medical treatment or those who married in the country)? Often, the relevant population can differ in subtle ways across surveys due to changes in survey methods over time. In some cases, it may be possible to reconstruct indicators in order to define them through time across a consistent population.

¬ *Recommendation: Record indicators in the database, where relevant and feasible, as both levels and rates.*

For some indicators, it will be important to determine whether changes in a rate occur because of changes in the numerator versus changes in the denominator or both. By accessing the underlying data that go into the calculation of a rate (i.e., the numerator and denominator), it is possible to gain a better understanding of why the rate is changing over time. When such data are not available, it is important to consider alternative explanations for patterns observed in an indicator over time.

¬ *Recommendation: Obtain, where possible and relevant, estimates of the standard errors associated with particular indicators.*

Up and down movements in the point estimates of a given indicator over time are not uncommon, but such movement may reflect, in part, underlying sampling variability when the indicator is based on sample data or other variability introduced in calculating the indicator. Ideally, standard errors would be available for all indicators that are not based on a complete enumeration of the population to construct the associated confidence interval. This allows for a determination as to whether variation over time in an indicator represents meaningful change or just statistical variability. Likewise, the significance of differences in an indicator across groups or data sources can be assessed as well. When such standard errors are not available, changes over time or other differences must be interpreted with caution.

## Database Architecture and Processing

As part of this project, we undertook a detailed examination of the database architecture, identifying the strengths and limitations of the current approach. Based on this assessment, we make some recommendations regarding a future database architecture designed to address the limitations we found and to enhance the accuracy, functionality, ease of use, and ease of maintenance of the database.

The prototype social indicators database is implemented in Lotus Notes/Domino, version 6.x. This software platform allows a great deal of flexibility in the content of individual records in a database. It also allows for a systematic structure in cataloging the individual records. The prototype, as currently implemented, takes advantage of both these features.

The principal features of the prototype fall into four categories:

- *Database structure:* The structure of the database takes advantage of the flexibility provided by the software platform. Individual records include both data and metadata documenting the data. The data generally consist of time series of given indicators. The metadata included in each record document the source and sometimes the algorithm used to compute a derived indicator. These individual records are stored in a rigidly structured hierarchy. This hierarchy allows for rapid access to indicators relevant to a particular narrow subject area.

- *Data entry:* Currently, data, largely from publications by the Planning Council, are entered manually into the database. However, nothing in the database design precludes automated data entry.

- *Data retrieval:* Data retrieval is facilitated by user-base familiarity with Lotus Notes. It is also facilitated by the hierarchical storage system used for the individual records.

- *Data manipulation:* Lotus Notes/Domino provides tools that a skilled programmer can use to manipulate the data. These tools require a great deal of familiarity with the underlying structure of the data, and thus are not suitable for most end users. End users would typically download the data and manipulate it using Microsoft® Excel® or other software packages.

In our assessment of the current prototype database, we noted several strengths of the implementation, as well as several weaknesses. This assessment informed our investigation of strategies for revising the database architecture to address the limitations of the prototype database.

The strengths include providing (1) a user-friendly platform with which the QSCFA user base is already familiar, the result of its current use of Lotus Notes/Domino in performing other routine tasks such as email; (2) a strict hierarchical organization that is clear and precise, allowing individual departments to readily access data that are pertinent to their areas of responsibility; (3) considerable flexibility in the storage of data and the associated metadata that documents the data; and (4) the ability to enhance and expand the database capabilities over time through extension packages (e.g., those that provide report-writing or graphics).

The limitations include (1) the use of manual data entry, which is both time-consuming and error-prone; (2) the strict hierarchical organization of the database, which makes it difficult to compare thematically similar indicators across a hierarchy; (3) the flexibility of the individual record format, which precludes ready manipulation of the data without human intervention or great ingenuity on the part of a programmer; and (4) the unstructured nature of the data, which leads to difficulty in performing computations. Note that the second and third examples are both strengths and limitations. These cases illustrate that some elements that are strengths within one context can in turn be weaknesses within another context.

Based on these observations regarding the strengths and weaknesses of the existing prototype, we make the following recommendations:

¬ *Recommendation: Establish standards for electronic data exchange.*

The vast majority of the indicators identified on this report are based on data published by the Planning Council, though some indicators will be based on data from other agencies as well. At present, such data are entered manually. This makes maintenance of the database laborious, time-consuming, and error-prone. Thus, we recommend that the QSCFA establish standards for electronic data exchange with the Planning Council and other agencies. We recommend adopting the non-proprietary XML standard for transmitting machine-readable databases, as XML is becoming the common representation language for document interchange over the Web. This would be in addition to any human-readable electronic provision of data by the Planning Council or other agencies (e.g., via Web pages.)

¬ *Recommendation: Use a dedicated database management system for storage, manipulation, and retrieval of data.*

Three of the limitations noted above are due largely to the nature of the software platform used to implement the prototype. While the characteristics of the native database of Lotus Notes/Domino make it a useful platform for creating prototype applications to demonstrate capabilities, these characteristics can lead to difficulty in a production environment. Thus, we recommend adopting a

DBMS for storage and manipulation of data using either a relational database management system (RDBMS) or a data warehouse.

¬ **Recommendation: Adopt a three-tiered client/server database architecture: client, application server or Web server, and database server.**

We recommend adopting a three-tiered client/server architecture to support the use of either the RDBMS or the data warehouse recommended above, and to provide more flexibility and functionality for the end users. The three tiers consist of (1) a client tier, which provides a graphical user interface (GUI) or Web browser; (2) an application server or Web server tier, which provides application programs or Web pages to act as intermediaries between the client and the database server and can provide access-control and other security measures; and (3) a database server tier, which includes the database management system. This is rapidly becoming the standard best practice for many Web applications. (The current prototype uses a two-tiered architecture, with Lotus Domino serving as both the database and application server, and Lotus Notes as the client.) The three-tiered database architecture is illustrated in Figure S.2.

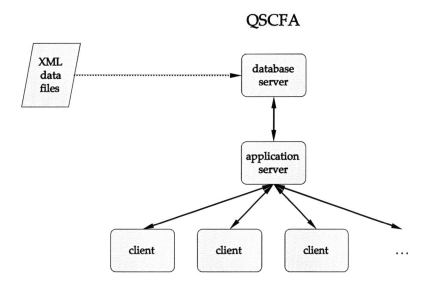

Figure S.2—Proposed Database Architecture

¬ *Recommendation: Implement the user interface of the database as a Web browser application using non-proprietary standards, rather than a Lotus Notes/Domino–specific application.*

This recommendation stems from two factors: (1) the desirability of using non-proprietary standards, and (2) the ease of integration with other Web-based resources. Non-proprietary standards are desirable in that they free the database from dependence upon any particular software manufacturer. This will aid in ensuring that the database can be migrated to newer and better environments as the state of the art improves. The ease of integration with other Web-based resources is useful in particular because of the stated intention of the Planning Council to provide a Web-based interface for the QSCFA indicators that they are tasked with producing.

¬ *Recommendation: Add a provision for ad hoc queries.*

The recommended list of indicators is our best assessment of the set of indicators that are currently needed by the QSCFA to execute its missions. However, the needs of the QSCFA may change over time, or new data or ways of looking at data may come to light. Thus, we recommend that in addition to providing the listed indicators, the system provide some mechanism for ad hoc queries. This will help to ensure that the database system will continue to be relevant into the future.

Our discussion of the database architecture also assesses the use of international classification and coding schemes. In this regard, we add one further recommendation:

¬ *Recommendation: Where appropriate, store the international standard classification numbers or codes used to refer to a particular indicator in a searchable field of the database.*

Currently, no general system for classifying all social indicators exists. However, there are classification systems for certain subsets of data, such as for national income accounts. This recommendation recognizes that there may be some indicators for which it is worthwhile to use existing classification and coding schemes to allow experts familiar with these schemes to access the data using this information.

## Strategic Actions for Future Database Implementation

In terms of the shorter-term focus on developing a social indicators database system, our analysis has highlighted a number of critical issues pertaining to the database content, the database indicators and their measurement, and the database architecture and processing. We conclude by recommending a series of strategic actions for the QSCFA to pursue in order to meet the short-term objective for the database.

¬ *Recommendation: Develop a solid understanding of the various sources of data, their sample coverage, measures available, and strengths and limitations.*

The case studies conducted for a subset of key indicators demonstrate that it is essential to understand the features of the major data sources that are used to construct indicators in the database. This project has made initial progress in this area but it was not designed to be comprehensive in assessing the full range of possible data sources. This recommendation is especially relevant for census and population-based surveys, which may be limited to coverage of specific populations (e.g., by nationality or age group) or the periodicity of the data collection, and where questions may deviate from international standards or vary over time. Similar issues may arise with administrative data or registries and vital statistics as well, where changes in how data were collected or recorded are important to ascertain.

¬ *Recommendation: Conduct a complete review of data gaps for the preferred list of indicators.*

With a solid understanding of the various sources of data and a prioritized list of indicators, it is possible to identify more clearly where gaps exist in the availability of the data needed to compute the desired list of indicators. Our assessment identified areas of likely gaps, but the project was not designed to definitively identify all gaps in the data. Among the gaps that stand out are those indicators that are typically available only through survey data and where survey data have not yet covered the relevant topics. For example, to our knowledge, there are no existing surveys that collect information on household debt or the anthropometric measurements (e.g., height and weight) needed to assess obesity and other measures of nutritional status among children and adults. In addition to these obvious gaps, in some cases data may exist to compute an indicator but a closer inspection of the quality of the data might suggest that the source of the data has key limitations. In other cases, the data may be available but for only one point in time and it might be desirable to update the information. Hence, in these cases, a more preferred source of data may be sought.

¬ *Recommendation: Identify indicators to examine in an in-depth review of measurements, data sources, and data quality.*

We recommend that QSCFA identify indicators that merit an in-depth review of conceptual measurement, measurement based on current data, and the consistency of measures over time and across data sources. Priority should be given to indicators relevant across multiple departments, indicators that are complex to measure in theory and in practice, and measures that might derive from multiple data sources (e.g., different surveys or the same survey over time). Our list of priorities for indicators that would merit in-depth review would include

- the fertility rate

- vital statistics on births and deaths and associated indicators derived from these data

- measures of employment outcomes, such as the distribution of employment by class, occupation, and industry

- measures of consumption, income, and poverty

- educational enrollment and attainment indicators

- health status and measures of health behaviors (e.g., smoking, drug use).

¬ *Recommendation: Determine whether some indicators must be recomputed to be consistent over time.*

For certain key indicators, where it is known that changes in data processing or data sources over the years make an indicator less comparable over time, the QSCFA should consider accessing the original data to recompute the indictor using consistent methods over time. This means that the QSCFA database may not match the official published value for a given indicator at any given point in time, but it would create a consistent indicator over time that can be used to assess progress.

¬ *Recommendation: Determine whether new data collection is required.*

Based on indicators that remain a priority but for which current data are not available or are not adequate, the QSCFA should assess the need for new data collection. This may take one of several forms:

- capturing administrative data or data from registries in new ways

- revising or adding questions or modules to existing population-based surveys of households or families, or surveys of businesses

- collecting entirely new survey data in special-purpose or general-purpose surveys, either cross-sectional or longitudinal.

Either the first or second type of data collection effort is likely to be less costly than the third, and therefore easier to implement in the short-term. As an example, questions on household debt may be added to future waves of the Household Expenditure and Income Survey (HEIS). Likewise, health questions and anthropometric measurements could be added to future rounds of the Family Health Survey (FHS). We return to the third option below.

¬ *Recommendation: Establish a formal mechanism for cooperation with the Planning Council in the implementation of the recommended database architecture.*

The working relationship of the QSCFA and the Planning Council is vital to the successful implementation of the database of indicators. One of the principal recommendations concerning the database architecture is that standards should be implemented for the electronic interchange of data between the Planning Council and the QSCFA. In addition, the QSCFA and the Planning Council should establish a mechanism for quality-assurance, maintenance, and updating of the source data for the indicators, as well as the appropriate methods to ensure data confidentiality and security.

## Long-Term Focus: Recommendations Regarding Microdata and Data Collection

As noted above, we identified longer-term objectives for the QSCFA database, beyond a social indicators database system: namely, having the data and capacity to analyze relationships between variables and policy impacts. While the main focus in the near-term is on the social indicators database system, we put forth one recommendation regarding the longer-term objective as well.

¬ *Recommendation: Pursue development of a database with detailed information on individuals or families and the physical and human capacity to analyze such data.*

The initial step would be to explore options for the QSCFA to begin to store and analyze the underlying microdata used to construct the social indicators. This first step would be relatively straightforward, provided that computing capacity and staff with expertise in data analysis are available. The second step would be to begin exploration of a new multipurpose survey, ideally one following the same households over time, to collect the specialized data needed to inform QSCFA decisionmaking. A multipurpose survey would allow analysis of multiple dimensions of family life in the same data source—economic data analyzed together with data on demographic behavior, health outcomes, human-capital investments, and other aspects of family decisionmaking. A survey that follows the same households and individuals over time would permit analyses of the dynamics of decisionmaking over time: marriage and divorce, labor force entry and exit, schooling investments, changes in health status, responses to economic shocks (e.g., death of a household member), and so on. Such data do not currently exist in Qatar and would be a tremendous asset for understanding a wide array of issues addressed by the QSCFA and its departments. In developing such a survey, it will be critical to develop protocols to ensure the privacy of individuals and families from which information is collected, including greater security provisions than what is required for a database of summary statistics. Such a survey would be a large undertaking, but ultimately a worthwhile investment in terms of improved knowledge of the well-being of families, women, children, youth, the elderly, and those with special needs in Qatar's rapidly changing economic, cultural, and social environment.

# Acknowledgments

We would like to thank Mr. Abdullah Nasser M. Al-Khalifa, the Secretary General of the Supreme Council for Family Affairs, for his support of this project. Dr. Lulwa A. Al-Misnad of the QSCFA governing board also helped define and launch the study. Mr. Abdulla Al-Abdul Malek, Manager of the QSCFA Information Technology Department, gave generously of his time in organizing meetings and providing information on the prototype social indicators database system. Dr. Kamil K. Al-Adhadh also provided valuable guidance and oversight of this project. Other QSCFA staff and staff of the Qatar Planning Council gave generously of their time as well. We also appreciate the constructive review of the draft report provided by Dr. Abdulilah Dewachi of the United Nations Economic and Social Commission for Western Asia (ESCWA).

Our RAND colleague Constantijn (Stan) Panis participated in the design and early phases of the project and we appreciate his contributions. We also benefited from thorough reviews of an earlier draft by our RAND colleague Julie DaVanzo and an anonymous reviewer. RQPI staff member Jihane Najjar provided valuable assistance to the project team. Administrative support was provided by RQPI staff member Nermin El-Mongi in Doha and RAND staff member Mechelle Wilkins in Arlington, Virginia.

# Abbreviations

| | |
|---|---|
| AF | Qatar Armed Forces |
| CPI | Consumer Price Index |
| DBMS | database management system |
| DOTS | directly observed treatment short course |
| DPT | diphtheria, Pertussis (whooping cough), and tetanus |
| EIS | executive information system |
| ESCWA | Economic and Social Commission for Western Asia, United Nations |
| FHS | Family Health Survey |
| GDI | gender-related development index |
| GEM | gender-empowerment measure |
| GUI | graphical user interface |
| HDI | Human Development Index |
| HEIS | Household Expenditure and Income Survey |
| HMC | Hamad Medical Corporation |
| HPI | Human Poverty Index |
| ICD | International Classification of Disease |
| ISIC | International Standard Industrial Classification |
| LAMP | Linux, Apache, MySQL, and PHP |
| LFS | Labour Force Survey |
| MCSAH | Ministry of Civil Service Affairs and Housing |
| MIA | Ministry of Interior Affairs |
| MOE | Ministry of Education |
| MoH | Ministry of Health |
| MPH | Ministry of Public Health |
| NHA | National Health Authority |
| ODA | Official Development Assistance |
| ODBC | open database connectivity |
| OLAP | online analytical processing |
| OLTP | online transaction processing |
| PC | Qatar Planning Council |
| PERL | Practical Extraction and Report Language |
| PHP | hypertext preprocessor |
| PPP | purchasing power parity |
| QF | Qatar Foundation |
| QNEDS | Qatar National Education Data System |

QSCFA Qatar Supreme Council for Family Affairs
R&D research and development
RDBMS relational database management system
RELAX Regular Language Description for XML
RQPI RAND-Qatar Policy Institute
SEC Supreme Education Council
SNA System of National Accounts
SOAP Simple Object Access Protocol
SQL structured query language
UNDP United Nations Development Programme
VS vital statistics
W3C World Wide Web Consortium

# 1. Introduction

The Qatar Supreme Council for Family Affairs (QSCFA) was established in 1998. The QSCFA is under the authority of His Highness the Emir and works in collaboration and coordination with the cabinet, the ministries, public corporations, and various councils and institutions. The QSCFA's vision is stated as follows:

> The Council aspires to see a Qatari family that is strong, coherent, stable, self-reliant, and proud of its Arab Islamic culture and identity. A family that is aware of its duties and responsibilities, whose members enjoy good health. A family unit that participates actively in building a society that is productive, open to the rest of the world and enjoys a stable and prosperous life. (QSCFA, undated brochure, p. 11)

To achieve this vision, the QSCFA is charged with reviewing and proposing legislation, promoting policies, adopting plans, implementing projects and programs, enhancing the role of national institutions, and disseminating information related to all aspects of family affairs in Qatar.

In support of its mission, the QSCFA maintains a series of nine goals, which are summarized in Table 1.1. These goals pertain to the role and care of families, the challenges facing families, the goals of international charters relating to family matters, the empowerment and participation of women in society and the labor market, the status of people with special needs, and the challenges facing youth.

This mission is achieved through six operating departments that focus on specific populations in Qatar: the family, women, children, youth, the elderly, and people with special needs. For each of these groups, a department within the QSCFA is tasked with reviewing programs and policies, developing plans for new activities, and implementing programs and monitoring their progress. Each department also has a corresponding committee of the Board of Directors. Table 1.1 shows the link between the nine goals and six departments, indicating that several goals have broad applicability to all departments, while others are central to only one department.

In support of its vision and specific goals, the QSCFA is developing a social indicators database system of which a prototype has already been developed. The database will help assess the well-being of families in Qatar and will provide essential information for planning for future activities, monitoring progress

Table 1.1—QSCFA Goals and Departments

| Goal | Department | | | | | |
|------|--------|-------|-------|-------|---------|------------------|
|      | Family | Women | Child | Youth | Elderly | Special Needs |
| To enhance the role of the family in society | | | | | | |
| To care for the family and strengthen its ties | | | | | | |
| To study the challenges facing the family and recommending suitable actions | | | | | | |
| To achieve goals stated in international charters relating to family affairs | | | | | | |
| To work for the empowerment of women and their participation in the social, political, and economic life | | | | | | |
| To improve the conditions of working women | | | | | | |
| To supervise the care for and rehabilitation of those with special needs | | | | | | |
| To coordinate the activities of national civic institutions and those of regional and international organizations | | | | | | |
| To study the challenges facing youth and suggest appropriate solutions in coordination with relevant state authorities | | | | | | |

NOTE: Shaded cells indicate a goal is relevant for a given department.
SOURCE: QSCFA (undated brochure, p. 12).

against departmental goals, and setting policy priorities. Since the mission of the QSCFA spans a diverse array of issues and there are multiple sources of data, a centralized database will provide an efficient mechanism for supporting the activities of the Council. It will also assist in coordinating work across departments that may have overlapping interests.

The purpose of this document is to provide final results of an analysis by the RAND-Qatar Policy Institute (RQPI) in support of this database effort. In this report, we focus in particular on the following questions:

- What are the goals of the database system and how do they relate to the objectives of the QSCFA?

- What indicators are best suited to support the goals of the database system and how should they be measured?

- Are data available to compute the indicators?

- What architecture will best support the database system?

To address these questions, we undertook a review of the QSCFA goals and the current mission and potential future activities of the QSCFA departments. As noted above, the QSCFA has developed a prototype database system. For this project, we studied the architecture and indicators included in the prototype database. In addition, we reviewed the major sources of data available to construct most of the indicators of interest.

Our report is organized as follows. Chapter Two provides an overview of the QSCFA social indicators database system, summarizing the objectives of the database system, the needs of the QSCFA users, and the general features of the database system. In Chapter Three, we turn to a discussion of the database indicators, providing an overview of data sources and recommended enhancements to the list of indicators already included in the prototype. In Chapter Four, we consider the architecture of the database system and outline objectives for the architecture. The architecture of the prototype database system and recommended changes are also reviewed. Chapter Five provides our recommendations for next steps and future directions of the QSCFA database system.

# 2. QSCFA Social Indicators Database System

We begin in this chapter by outlining the objectives of a social indicators database system for the QSCFA. We consider both immediate objectives, as well as potential longer-term goals for utilizing data at the Council. We then review the focus of the six main departments at the QSCFA and identify the types of data relevant for its current mission and potential future goals. Finally, we provide a broad overview of the database content, including the major topic areas to be covered and the types of information to be recorded.

## Objectives for the Database System

The database system may have both short-term and longer-term benefits for the work of the QSCFA. We begin by outlining the goals of the database development project in the near future and conclude by discussing some potential longer-term considerations. These short-term and longer-term features of the database system and their relationship to QSCFA objectives are summarized in Figure 2.1.

### Short-Term Objectives

The immediate goal of the QSCFA database development project is to create a database of summary measures that are relevant to the activities of the QSCFA. The indicators in the database would support the analysis, planning, and decisionmaking of the various QSCFA departments, notably those focusing on the family, women, children, youth, the elderly, and people with special needs. With this objective in mind, the database system may be used to:

- *Track progress in a given domain or for a given outcome.* An indicator, ideally consistently measured across years, can be tracked over time to determine whether change in the indicator is favorable or unfavorable. Multiple indicators in a given domain, such as family well-being, health, or the labor force, can be compared and contrasted.

- *Compare alternative measures of a given indicator.* In some cases, indicators may be measured in more than one way. Variants of an indicator may be stored in the database and compared at a point in time

6

or trends can be compared over time. Comparisons may also be made across different data sources or statistical reports.

- *Examine indicators for population subgroups or geographic areas.* Some indicators may be stored for population subgroups such as women or men, people disaggregated by age, or for Qataris and non-Qataris. Indicators may be compared across groups or for a given group with the population average.

- *Generate statistics for QSCFA reports or for international agency reports.* The information stored in the social indicators database system may be used to generate statistics for use in QSCFA reports, including reports that are updated on a periodic basis or specialized reports on a given topic. The indicators can include those required to meet international reporting requirements, such as the indicators included in the United Nations Development Programme (UNDP) *Human Development Report* (see UNDP, 2003).

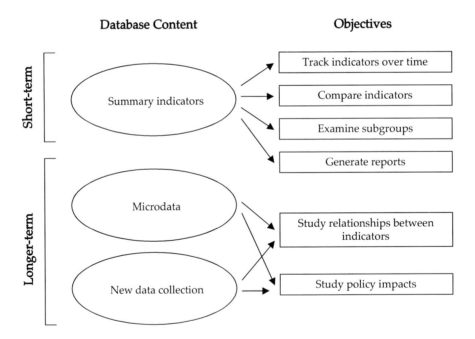

Figure 2.1—Relationship Between Database Content and Objectives in the Short-Term and Longer-Term

Thus, the database system needs to be flexible enough to

- *Accommodate multiple indicators.* Given the diverse activities of the QSCFA departments, a wide array of indicators are relevant. In many cases, the same indicator will be of interest to more than one department. And the same indicator may be measured in more than one way.

- *Store indicators for multiple years.* In order to monitor historical patterns and track future progress, the database system will need to store information on a given indicator over time. Since all indicators will not be available for the same time periods, the database system needs to be flexible to account for different periodicities across indicators.

- *Allow indicators to be analyzed as levels or rates.* Many indicators may be measured as both a level (e.g., the number of women in Qatar) and as a proportion (e.g., the fraction of the population in Qatar that is female). In this example, the latter figure is defined as the former divided by the total population, another potential indicator. The database system may record some measures as both levels and rates, or alternatively store only the information in levels but calculate rates using appropriate numerators and denominators.

- *Record or derive indicators in aggregate and for disaggregated groups or geographic areas.* Several of the QSCFA departments focus on specific population subgroups such as women, children, and youth. For many aspects of planning and decisionmaking, it is relevant to compare outcomes for one group against those of another (e.g., women versus men, groups defined by age), or for individuals in one geographic area of the country versus another.

- *Add new fields for each indicator over time or add new indicators over time.* The information needs of the QSCFA departments are not static, but change over time as new priorities are identified and new policy questions arise. Thus, the social indicators database system needs to be flexible enough to allow new indicators to be added over time, or for new fields for each indicator to be incorporated as needed.

In the short term, for most cases, the indicators stored in the database will be based on data collected by other agencies in the Qatari public sector, such as the Planning Council or other government departments, and the QSCFA will not be involved directly in generating the summary measures. The potential sources of data are discussed in Chapter Three.

## *Potential Longer-Term Objectives*

While these uses and features of the social indicators database system will support the ongoing needs of the QSCFA, over a longer horizon, the database needs may be expanded in order to provide even greater support of analysis, planning, and decisionmaking. The first step toward developing effective policy recommendations is to identify trends or gaps between current achievement and targets. The next steps are to (1) determine the causes of trends or gaps, (2) identify subpopulations that are particularly affected, and (3) formulate policy interventions that efficiently and effectively help the populations of interest. These next steps are likely to require analytic tools and data that a database of summary statistics may not necessarily provide. In particular, we can anticipate two future directions for the QSCFA in terms data generation, manipulation, and consumption.

First, in addition to storing summary measures in a database of indicators, the QSCFA would benefit in the future from storing the underlying data used to generate these indicators. Assuming that the QSCFA employs sufficient staff to analyze such data, the QSCFA departments would have even greater flexibility to generate the types of data needed for decisionmaking. The underlying data may include census or survey data, vital statistics data, or administrative data. Access to the detailed data (microdata) used to generate summary indicators will permit analyses that look at the relationship between indicators (e.g., the relationship between family income and women's employment). Such analyses can begin to uncover the association between different indicators, and in some cases, the causal relationship between indicators. Such data may also support studies of the relationships between specific policies and the outcomes they are designed to influence.

Second, in addition to being a consumer of data generated by other public-sector departments, the QSCFA may become a producer of data. Given the diverse program areas covered by the QSCFA and the unique data needs of the Council, in some cases, the data needed to support decisionmaking will not currently exist. This may be because the information is not currently collected (e.g., it is not covered in any survey or administrative data source), or it is not collected in the way needed to support the desired analyses (e.g., information on the topics of interest are not collected in the same data source or over the needed time period). For example, many of the policy issues relevant for the QSCFA cover multiple domains of family life: demographic decisions (e.g., marriage, divorce, childbearing), economic decisions (e.g., labor force behavior, spending behavior), or health behavior (e.g., health status, health care utilization). Most data sources, such as censuses, labor force surveys, or household budget surveys, do not contain information on these multiple domains simultaneously. As another example, many aspects of family life take place over time and therefore outcomes are inherently dynamic. Behavior that changes over time is ideally analyzed using longitudinal data that tracks the same individuals or families through time. Such longitudinal data are often not collected in larger-scale surveys but can be collected in smaller, more intensive surveys. Thus, it may be that in the future, new data collection is required in support of policymaking at the Council.

In sum, to formulate effective policy recommendations, a database with information on individuals or families is needed. In addition to such macro-level information as social indicators, thorough analysis requires micro-level information on individuals' health, education, living arrangements, income, and so on. Individual-level information can reveal the sources of lagging progress. For example, suppose a social indicator on school enrollment among 15-year-olds shows that the actual enrollment rate is lower than the target rate. Individual-level information can identify which youths are not in school and what their family circumstances are. Perhaps some are not in school because they need to help their needy parents; perhaps children in poor families need to work; or perhaps children of poorly educated parents are more likely to leave school. Only individual-level information can reveal such patterns and help formulate effective policy interventions.

Clearly, the development of an integrated system of individual-level data collection, storage, and analysis is a long-term issue, and the collection and maintenance of a database with individual-level data go beyond the initial objective of developing a database with social indicators. We mention these potential longer-term objectives here because a sketch of an "ideal" information system provides focus for the first stage of the development of the social indicators database system. These potential objectives are also useful because they help to avoid early decisions that may hamper the achievement of long-term goals later.

## Database Users

The main consumers or users of the QSCFA database will be QSCFA staff in the six main departments of the Council, namely the departments that focus on the family, women, children, youth, the elderly, and people with special needs. The data will also be useful for the work of the committees associated with each of the departments.

It is worth noting, given the overlapping goals of the departments and the domains they cover, that there will not be a one-to-one correspondence between

QSCFA departments and subsets of social indicators. Many indicators will be relevant to more than one department: For example, many measures that pertain to the health of the family will also be relevant to women, children, or youth.

## Family

The Department of Family focuses on a range of issues relevant to Qatari and non-Qatari families. At present, these include topics such as parental involvement in schools, social development centers, the provision of benefits and other services under the social security program, marital stability and the well-being of families and children, and living arrangements of families and family well-being. Policy considerations include changes to the social security program eligibility rules and benefit structure and related laws affecting pensioners, revisions to personal status laws governing civil rights and family affairs, and changes in housing law. Given the breadth of the policy issues covered by this department, a wide array of indicators are relevant to most population subgroups.

## Women

The objective of the Department of Women is to empower women and increase their participation in the economy and public life. The department is interested in general indicators of women's status, social status indicators, education and labor indicators, and indicators of participation in civil society. Current areas of focus include assessing the status of women's health, compensation for women in cases of wrongful death, women's rights under civil law and status law, women in high positions of authority, women in self-employment, and the well-being of Qatari women married to non-Qatari men. The department is also interested in the comparative status of women and men in Qatar. This subject was the focus of the statistical portrait published in 2004, titled *Women and Men in Qatar* (QSCFA, 2004).

## Children

The Department of Childhood focuses on advancing and promoting the well-being of children from birth to age 17 in the areas of child health and development, childhood conditions, and children's rights. The areas of current focus include children's rights in the schools, pre-primary education, violence against children, childhood obesity, children with HIV/AIDS, children living under difficult circumstances (e.g., those without nationality or with anonymous parents), and the economic circumstances of families with children. Another major focus is meeting the international reporting requirements of the United Nations, such as those arising from the 1999 Convention on the Rights of the Child. Typically, information is provided on the appropriate methodology to use in calculating indicators submitted to these international bodies. For many indicators that focus on children, it is relevant to consider differences between girls and boys.

## Youth

The Department of Youth generally covers the status of individuals age 18 to 35, essentially the young-adult years. The department covers a range of issues concerning the social, economic, and health status of youth. Current topics include the democratic movement in the Gulf States; youth employment and unemployment; youth employed in private business; enrollment, field of study, and attainment in higher education; the transition to marriage and marriage supports; and the transition to divorce. Issues of rising importance include substance abuse by young adults, the prevalence of HIV/AIDS in this population, and accidental deaths among youth.

## Elderly

The Department of Elderly is broadly concerned with the social, economic, and health status of the older population—generally those over age 50—and other aspects of their environment. Current issues concerning the elderly include the provision of government social and health services, the social security program, elderly living arrangements and economic well-being, the timing of retirement and the activities of older retired persons, health and disability among the older population, and the transfer of time and financial support between the generations.

## People with Special Needs

The Department of Special Needs aims to promote the quality of life of people in Qatar with special needs due to the total or partial loss of physical or mental abilities. There are a number of important issues that are the focus of the department. Key issues currently being addressed involve the inclusion of those with special needs in the education sector, participation of the disabled in the labor market, marriage and family life among those with special needs, and improving the quality of services received by this population. Relevant policy issues include early intervention (e.g., birth to age five) for those with special needs, programs providing financial support to those with special needs (e.g., social security, social care), and employment law with respect to the disabled (e.g., laws requiring employers to hire a specified fraction of disabled workers). Given the diverse array of disabilities affecting those with special needs, it is often relevant to consider more detailed subpopulations in addressing any of these topics.

## Overview of Database Content

In this section, we provide a broad overview of the ideal content of the social indicators database system, including the subject domains as well as fields specific to each indicator.

### Subject Domains

Given the breadth and depth of the issues facing the users of the QSCFA database, it is natural that the subjects covered by the database will be equally comprehensive. The following broad subject domains correspond to the data needs of one or more QSCFA departments:[1]

- *Population.* This domain covers basic demographic information concerning the size and composition of the population and factors associated with population change (e.g., births, deaths, migration).

- *Economy.* This is a broad domain that captures aspects of the macroeconomy (e.g., gross national income, indicators of overall economic growth, inflation rates, and so on), as well as aspects of components of the economy, such as the labor market and other markets for goods and services.

- *Family life.* This domain concerns all aspects of family life, such as marriage and divorce, living arrangements, intergenerational relationships, and other aspects of family functioning. The economic status of families (e.g., family income and sources of income) is also included.

---

[1] In this discussion, we do not include non-data elements such as documents that are stored in the database as reference material for various international conventions and other international and domestic laws. These data elements are documents rather than social indicators.

- *Education.* This domain encompasses aspects of the production and consumption of education across all age groups, starting with preschool education and continuing through adult education and training. Measures of literacy and educational attainment are included as well.

- *Health and nutrition.* This domain covers aspects of health and nutritional status of the population as a whole and of relevant subgroups. Factors that affect health and nutrition, such as health-related behaviors (e.g., smoking, substance use), the consumption of health care, and food consumption, are also included.

- *Environment.* This domain includes all aspects of the environment that affect families in Qatar, including air, water, and sanitation.

- *Civil and political life.* This domain captures a range of topics specific to participation in civil society and in political life, including the role of media and communications, political participation, and the rights and laws that apply to civic and political life.

- *Safety and security.* This domain pertains to those aspects that affect the safety and security of the population, whether as individual citizens or collectively as a society.

- *Statutes.* This domain encompasses various conventions, laws, and other documents that are relevant for the mission of the QSCFA. These database elements are documents rather than indicators.

### Fields Specific to Each Indicator

Each indicator in the database should have a number of fields relevant to that indicator. These include the following:

- *Indicator label and definition.* Each indicator should have a short label as well as a longer label with a more detailed definition. For example, "Labor force participation rate" would be the short label that corresponds to the longer label, "Percentage of the working-age population that is working or actively looking for work."

- *Population unit.* Various fields should identify what the population unit is for each indicator. For example, the unit may be the entire population or only Qataris and non-Qataris. Indicators may be specific to men or women, age groups, or population groups defined by geographic region. Since the data may be disaggregated at various levels, a separate field will be required for each possible level of disaggregation (e.g., nationality, sex, age, region).

- *Date.* The date of measurement for a specific indicator should be included. Since the time period of measurement may vary (e.g., a given month in a specific year, or the entire year), the database should be flexible enough to capture different types of dates.

- *Unit of measure.* As noted earlier, some indicators may be measured in levels while others may be measured in percentage terms. Thus, the database should record the specific unit of measurement for an indicator.

- *Source data.* The source of the data should be recorded, such as whether the information was provided by another agency based on a specific survey or administrative data source, reported in a specific publication (page or table number should be given), calculated from other data in the database, or calculated from other data outside the database.

- *Methodological notes.* In some cases, the measurement of a given indicator will be straightforward. In other cases, it will be more complex. For example, some indicators will be the ratio of two numbers, while others will be based on a complex computation using microdata. The database should record information about the methodology used to generate a given indicator.

- *Other fields.* Other fields should record additional key information, such as which QSCFA departments are interested in the indicator, whether the indicator is a high priority for measurement, and whether the indicator is required for reporting to international agencies or for QSCFA reports. Other fields can record miscellaneous notes or reference information, such as aspects of data quality.

# 3. QSCFA Database Indicators

This chapter focuses on the indicators in the QSCFA database system. We begin by briefly reviewing the main sources of data available for constructing indicators. This list is not necessarily comprehensive but is intended to represent the major sources of data available. We then turn to a discussion of our recommendations for indicators for the database in nine broad domains corresponding to those listed in Chapter Two: population, economy, family life, education, health and nutrition, environment, civil and political life, safety and security, and statutes. These recommendations are based on a review of the list of indicators included in the current prototype database system, as well as further discussion with QSCFA staff about their future data needs. Notably, some indicators are included even though there may not yet be data available to measure them.

## Sources of Data

Given the array of indicators that are of potential interest for the QSCFA social indicators database system, there are a number of data sources from which these indicators can be drawn. Table 3.1 lists these potential sources, first for data that come from administrative sources, second for those that come from censuses or surveys, and third for those that are compiled in database systems.

**National accounts.** National accounts data, compiled by the Planning Council in Qatar, provide information on the economic stocks and flows of the national economy. This is the source of information about gross domestic product (GDP) and other measures of aggregate economic activity, as well as information about components of GDP, such as gross national income, consumption, and international trade (exports and imports). National accounts data also provide information on price trends.

**Vital statistics.** Vital statistics data on births, deaths, marriages, and divorces are typically available on a monthly and annual basis. These vital statistics are collected by various ministries (e.g., births and deaths by the Ministry of Health [MoH]; marriages and divorces by the Ministry of Justice) and compiled by the Planning Council. The data are often reported for subgroups defined by sex, age (when relevant), nationality, and municipality.

16

Table 3.1—Potential Sources of Data for Indicators

| Data Source or Survey | Producer | Year |
|---|---|---|
| **Administrative Data** | | |
| National accounts | Planning Council | Varies |
| Vital statistics | Planning Council | Monthly and/or annual data |
| Registries | Various ministries | Varies |
| Administrative records | Various ministries | Varies |
| **Survey Data** | | |
| Qatar Population and Housing Census | Planning Council | 1986, 1997, 2004 |
| Qatar Labour Force Survey | Planning Council | April 2001 |
| Qatar Household Expenditure and Income Survey | Planning Council | 1988, 2001 |
| Qatar Family Health Survey | Ministry of Health and Planning Council | 1986, 1998 |
| **Database Systems** | | |
| Qatar National Education Data System | Supreme Education Council | 2004, 2005 |

**Registries.** Other information is recorded by various ministries in the form of registries. For example, information is available on the population with special needs based on those who have registered at centers that provide services to this population.

**Administrative records.** Administrative records maintained by various ministries and public or private entities can be another source of data for a wide array of indicators. For example, information on the infrastructure of the education system is maintained by the Supreme Education Council (SEC) and the Ministry of Education (MOE), while data on the health care system is collected by the MoH, the National Health Authority (NHA), and the Hamad Medical Corporation (HMC).[1]

**Population and housing census.** The first national census in Qatar was conducted in March 1986. A second census took place in March 1997, while the most recent

---

[1] The NHA was previously called the Ministry of Public Health (MPH). Historical health indicators, including data sources we reference in this document, would have been under the purview of the MPH.

census was completed in March 2004. The next census is expected in 2010. The 2004 census was a complete enumeration of Qatari families based only on a long-form instrument. Information on non-Qatari families was collected for a sample using a shorter instrument. The 1986 and 1997 censuses provide a complete enumeration of all households in Qatar regardless of nationality. Each census included a building census, along with the collection of data on households and individuals. The long-form instrument includes basic demographic information on all individuals (age, sex, nationality, marital status, and education level), as well as labor force data, internal migration, fertility, marriage, and income.

**Labour Force Survey (LFS).** The most recent household LFS was conducted in 2001 for a sample of about 2,000 households (Qatar Planning Council, 2002). The Planning Council expects to collect these data again for a new sample in 2006 and annually thereafter. The household survey collects basic demographic information (like the census), along with details on labor force activity. Other employment information is available from annual establishment data.

**Household Expenditure and Income Survey (HEIS).** The HEIS (sometimes called the Family Budget Survey) was collected in 1988 and 2000–2001. The Planning Council expects to conduct this survey every five years in the future. It is a sample survey of about 2,000 households with one respondent per household who provides information on expenditures and income sources and amounts.

**Family Health Survey (FHS).** The FHS was conducted in 1986 and 1998 and may be collected every five years in the future. The most recent survey, conducted as part of the Gulf Family Health Survey program, interviewed a sample of Qatari households only, though the sample also included non-Qatari domestic staff residing in the sampled households (Al-Jaber and Farid, 2000). For the approximately 4,200 households interviewed in 1998, information was collected for all individuals on health status, health history, and health care utilization; for ever-married women under age 50 on marriage, fertility and fertility preferences, prenatal and postnatal care, infant feeding, and contraceptive use; and for children under age 5 on child care and vaccinations (for children ages 12 to 23 months only).

**Qatar National Education Data System (QNEDS).** One potential resource for the QSCFA in compiling education indicators is QNEDS, which is being developed by the SEC in collaboration with RQPI. QNEDS focuses on data for public, new independent, and private Arabic schools. (Private non-Arabic schools are not covered.) For these institutions, new survey data have been collected on the schools, students, parents, teachers, principals, school administrators, and school social workers in 2004 and 2005, with plans for an annual update. Information compiled by the MOE from administrative data is also included in the database.

## Recommended Indicators

Table 3.2 provides a summary of our recommendations with respect to specific indicators for nine broad domains: population, economy, family life, education, health and nutrition, environment, civil and political life, safety and security, and statutes.[2] The list of indicators builds upon a set of desired indicators originally compiled in March 2004 by the QSCFA for its prototype database. For a subset of these indicators, data have already been collected and entered into the prototype database. For the list we present here, some indicators identified for the prototype database have been excluded based on our judgment of their relevance for the QSCFA mission, while new indicators have been added. In some cases, the additions reflect new priorities of the QSCFA departments and staff identified during our discussions. In Table 3.2, indicators that were not listed in the QSCFA prototype database as of March 2004 are shown in italics (second column).

Within each broad domain, specific indicators are grouped within subdomains and are listed using a short title, as well as a longer definition. Each indicator is associated with an alphanumeric code that can be used to reference the indicator. These codes, sequential within each broad domain, are for internal purposes only and do not correspond to any external classification scheme, as discussed further in Chapter Four.

For complex indicators, the definition includes relevant citations that provide more detail on the measurement of the indicator. In most cases, however, the indicators are simple counts or ratios. When the definition of an indicator involves the ratio of two numbers, we do not explicitly state that the ratio should be multiplied by 100 to derive a percentage, or divided by 1,000 to obtain the rate per 1000 persons (or the equivalent calculation for some other population-based rate). Such additional manipulations of the data are assumed. We also assume that international data standards are followed in the calculation of national accounts measures (see United Nations Statistics Division, 1993), and that such international classification standards as the International Standard Industrial

---

[2] Note that we have not organized our list of indicators by QSCFA department, but rather by the broad domains listed in Chapter Two. This is because many indicators will be of interest to more than one department.

Classification of all Economic Activities (see United Nations Statistics Division, 2002) are followed, as well.

In addition, the measurement unit is stated for each indicator shown in Table 3.2, primarily to designate indicators that are measured as levels versus rates. In some cases, we recommend storing both. If an indicator was included in the prototype list of indicators as of March 2004 but we recommend adding another unit of measurement (e.g., levels in addition to percent), that measurement unit is shown in italics.

When it is desirable to record an indicator for subgroups (e.g., life expectancy for men and women), we indicate the subgroup measurement through the next series of columns of Table 3.2. The following subgroups are specified with an "X" in each of six columns: sex (male, female), age (age groups defined typically by 5- or 10-year age intervals), nationality (Qatari, non-Qatari), special needs (special needs population and possibly subgroups of this population), family headship status (male-headed families versus female-headed families, or families defined by the presence and ages of children) or marital status (married, separated, divorced, widowed, unmarried, or combinations of these categories), and geography (urban versus rural or different regions as defined by the Planning Council).

The table also indicates the QSCFA departments that are likely to benefit from each indicator, again with an "X" in one of six columns corresponding to each of the departments. By inference, given the link between an indicator and the department(s) that will benefit from this indicator shown in Table 3.2, the indicators are also linked to the goals of the QSCFA listed in Table 1.1 in Chapter One.

The next column records the expected source of data. When one or more sources for the indicator are known, we list those sources. When a data source is not known or known not to be available, we list the potential source of data in italics.[3] This may be the government entity by which we expect the data would be maintained, or a potential new data source such as a new survey. In some cases, we indicate that we expect that the indicator would be available through administrative records maintained in the public or private sector. The source of data will be the principle determinant of the frequency with which the indicator is available. In most cases, the indicators will be available on an annual basis.

---

[3] The uncertainty about data sources arises because the scope of this project did not allow us to undertake a complete investigation of all possible data sources.

Some indicators come from data sources that are collected less frequently (e.g., the census) and will therefore be available on a less frequent basis.

The next two columns pertain to the UNDP *Human Development Report* (see UNDP, 2003). We indicate with an "X" in the first column those indicators that are included in the annual UNDP report. The next column indicates whether the report actually had a value for the indicator for Qatar in the most recent year. In many cases, an indicator is not reported in the UNDP *Human Development Report* for Qatar, either because the indicator is not relevant for a high-income country such as Qatar, or the data are not available to calculate the indicator.

Finally, the last column indicates the priority we recommend assigning to each indicator. The rankings range from 1, the highest priority, to 4, the lowest priority. Indicators with a rank of 1 are most relevant for the QSCFA's mission and goals, and for the objectives of the designated departments. These are typically indicators that are internationally recognized as important social indicators, and indicators that are included in the UNDP *Human Development Report*. The data are also readily available to compute the indicator, or the indicator is routinely made available by the indicated sources. Indicators with a rank of 2 are somewhat less relevant for the QSCFA's mission, but are expected to be available from current data sources. Alternatively, they may be highly relevant indicators but they are ranked lower-priority because the data are not yet readily available, so additional effort will be required to bring them on line. Indicators with a rank of 3 follow a similar logic, being even less relevant for the QSCFA's mission or even more difficult to obtain. Finally, those ranked 4 are the least relevant for the QSCFA's mission and the context in Qatar. Based on these rankings, we recommend incorporating indicators with a rank of 1 first, followed by those ranked 2 and 3 as resources allow and the data become available. Those with a rank of 4 would have the last priority and should be included only if the data can be obtained, subject to current resource constraints.

To further highlight the link between the indicators and the QSCFA's mission, Table 3.3 denotes which QSCFA goals (cited earlier in Table 1.1) are served by each indicator. The first three goals pertain to improving family well-being and there is little to differentiate indicators according to the three goals. Thus, those goals are combined in the first column. Goals 4, 5, 6, 7, and 9 are shown in the following five columns. The eighth goal, pertaining to coordination of activities across national institutions, regional organizations, and international entities, is less reliant on data so we have excluded this goal from the list. Thus, the goals as summarized in Table 3.3 are as follows:

- Goals 1–3 (Family well-being): To enhance the role of the family in society, to care for the family and strengthen its ties, and to study the challenges facing the family and recommending suitable actions

- Goal 4 (Charters on family affairs): To achieve goals stated in international charters relating to family affairs

- Goal 5 (Women's empowerment): To work for the empowerment of women and their participation in social, political, and economic life

- Goal 6 (Women's work): To improve the conditions of working women

- Goal 7 (Support those with special needs): To supervise the care for and rehabilitation of those with special needs

- Goal 9 (Youth challenges): To study the challenges facing youth and suggest appropriate solutions in coordination with relevant state authorities.

We now review the main recommendations associated with each domain.

## Population (P-series)

The population domain (coded P-xxx) contains indicators that pertain to population structure, population growth, and life expectancy. With a few exceptions, these are indicators already included in the prototype database. Recommended new indicators include the population distribution (P-002) by five of the six subgroups (headship status is excluded), the general birth rate (P-013), and cause-specific mortality rates (P-017). Other new indicators were recommended by QSCFA staff in our discussions (e.g., the dependency ratio [P-004], median age [P-005], the median age at first birth [P-015], and population density [P-006]). For some of the existing indicators, we recommend more explicitly recording information by subgroup, often defined by sex, age, or nationality. Some indicators would be specific to the special needs population.

As indicated, many of these population measures are relevant for most, if not all, QSCFA departments. We would expect most of these indicators to come from vital statistics or other registries, the census, or possibly intercensal estimates based on other population surveys (e.g., FHS). As such, they will generally be available annually (those derived from vital statistics or intercensal estimates) or less frequently for other sources (e.g., census). About half of these indicators are included in the *Human Development Report* and values exist in each case for

Qatar. All of the indicators are assigned a priority of 1 because they are key indicators and are readily available from existing data sources.

## *Economy (E-series)*

The economy domain (coded E-xxx) covers a broad array of indicators that capture the macroeconomy (e.g., overall economic activity, international trade, human development indicators, development assistance, and technology), along with labor market indicators (e.g., labor force, employment, and unemployment). For the first group of indicators, most are already included in the database, though several new indicators are included as recommended by the QSCFA (e.g., gross national income [E-009], consumption [E-010], investment and savings as a share of GDP [E-011 and E-012, respectively], and the GDP implicit price deflator [E-017]). Most of these indicators are relevant primarily for the Department of Family. Most would come from national accounts data or data compiled by the United Nations and would be available on an annual basis.[4]

The indicators in the technology domain include several indicators (E-039 to E-048) recently recommended for collection by the World Summit on the Information Society convened by the United Nations Economic and Social Commission for Western Asia (ESCWA) (ESCWA, 2005).[5] These indicators measure the penetration of various information and communication technologies at the population, household, business, and employee levels. These indicators are generally not available in Qatar at present, but could be potentially derived from sources of private- or public-sector administrative data, population-based censuses or surveys, business censuses or surveys, and labor force surveys.

Many of these economy indicators are included in the *Human Development Report*, though values for Qatar are not always recorded (e.g., on debt service [E-013 and E-014], foreign direct investment [E-015 and E-016], and measures of trade and development assistance [E-020, E-021, E-025, and E-032]). Among the Human Development Indicators reported in the *Human Development Report*, only the Human Development Index (HDI) (E-026) has a value for Qatar.[6] These

---

[4] Note that a number of the indicators are traditionally measured in PPP (purchasing power parity) U.S. dollars. PPP is a rate of exchange that accounts for price differences across counties (see UNDP, 2004). One PPP U.S. dollar has the same purchasing power in the Qatar economy as a dollar in the United States.

[5] The list of recommended indicators by the ESCWA summit is more extensive than the list of indicators we have included in Table 3.2 (see ESCWA, 2005). We focus on the core indicators that are likely to be most readily available in Qatar and of greatest interest given the mission of the QSCFA.

[6] We have dropped the indicator "Human Development Index Trend," included in the prototype database, since this is merely a time series of the HDI, which is already included as an indicator and should be recorded for all available years.

various economic indicators receive a priority ranking of 1 or 2, based primarily on the ease with which data are expected to be available. In some cases, these indicators are less directly relevant for the mission and goals of the QSCFA (e.g., measures of trade activity, debt service, and investment flows), so they receive a rank of 2.

In terms of the labor force indicators (E-052 to E-075), we designate three subdomains: labor force, employment, and unemployment. Typically, the labor force is defined as the sum of those working and those actively looking for work (i.e., the unemployed). The labor force is also known as the economically active population. For the total economically active population (labor force) and its two components (employed and unemployed), we recommend collecting information on counts (e.g., the size of the labor force) and rates (e.g., the labor force participation rate equal to the labor force divided by the population). We have also included a measure of discouraged workers to capture those who are willing and able to work but who have given up actively searching for work (E-074 and E-075). In addition, for these three components (labor force, employed, and unemployed), we recommend indicators specific to subgroups defined by sex, age, nationality, special needs, headship or marital status, and geography. For example, the labor force participation rate of women defined by marital status or the presence or ages of children would be relevant subgroups to incorporate. All six departments are likely to be interested in these labor market indicators for the population as a whole or for specific subgroups (e.g., data on women's labor market activity for the Department of Women, and data on youth labor market activity for the Department of Youth). We expect that these indicators can be constructed from the LFS and therefore will be available on the same periodicity as the LFS (i.e., potentially more frequently in the future).

In the case of employment data, we recommend several new indicators (E-059 to E-066) that consider different groups of the employed defined by sector of employment (i.e., public sector versus private sector), class of employment (i.e., wage workers versus self-employed workers), industry (i.e., broad industry groups or specific industries), and occupation (i.e., broad occupation groups or specific occupations). In each case, the decomposition of the employed would be recorded both in levels (i.e., numbers) and as a percentage distribution. These indicators are relevant for several of the current priorities at the QSCFA (e.g., private-sector employment among youth). Again, we expect that these indicators can be measured in the LFS.

These labor force indicators are generally not included in the *Human Development Report*, other than basic indicators such as employment and unemployment rates. We assign the highest priority to these indicators pertaining to the labor force, employed, and unemployed. They have broad relevance to the mission of the QSCFA and can be readily measured in the LFS.

## Family Life (F-series)

The family life domain (coded F-xxx) captures aspects of family structure and composition, marriage and divorce, housing characteristics, poverty and income, consumption, and social support. Almost all of the indicators in this domain are currently included in the prototype database in some form, though several new indicators were included at the recommendation of the QSCFA (e.g., orphaned children [F-004], household debt [F-038], and beneficiaries of Zakat [obligatory charitable duty] [F-042]).[7] In several cases, we recommend including information on counts as well as rates, and we recommend collecting data by relevant subgroups, particularly those that have to do with family headship status or living arrangements. As an example, we note that information on the number and share of the population in various marital states (married, separated, divorced, widowed, never married) (F-008 to F-013) should be calculated for the population as a whole and also for subgroups defined by sex, age, and nationality, and for those with special needs. This allows for the examination of marriage patterns across age cohorts, such as the fraction that remains unmarried at successively older ages. In terms of household types and living arrangements, examples that could be examined include those defined by the existence and number of adults and children (e.g., single adult with no children, single adult with children, etc.) or by the absence or presence of multiple generations.

We also recommend several new indicators, including the number of households (F-001), the population (level and rate) in polygamous marriages (F-010), and household distribution by tenure (i.e., ownership) type (F-014). We also recommend including the UNDP Human Poverty Index (HPI-2) (F-022) in place of the HPI-1, since the former is relevant for high-income countries while the latter is more appropriate for low-income countries.[8] The HPI-2 is not currently reported for Qatar in the *Human Development Report* but it could be

---

[7] A recommended indicator for the average age at the time of remarriage was not included because the incidence of remarriage is so low that it would be difficult to have sufficient data to calculate the indicator properly. In particular, data from the FHS indicate that 94 percent of Qatari women marry only once, and of those who divorce, under half (44 percent) remarry (Al-Jaber and Farid, 2000).

[8] We have also omitted two other measures of low income that are in the prototype database: Namely, the fraction of the population that lives under $1 a day or $2 a day is included in the UNDP *Human Development Report*. These are indicators that are less relevant for a high-income country like Qatar, so we recommend that they not be included in the QSCFA database.

constructed from existing data sources following the UNDP methodology (see UNDP, 2004, p. 260).

Again, many of these indicators are likely to be of interest to multiple departments within the QSCFA, given their current priorities. In terms of data sources, these various family life indicators may be constructed from the census, LFS, FHS, HEIS, and other sources indicated in Table 3.2. Thus, the frequency of the data will depend upon the intervals between these survey sources. The measure of average household debt (F-038) would require new data collection as no surveys in Qatar, to our knowledge, collect information on household assets and debts. A subset of the measures in the poverty and income categories are reported in the *Human Development Report*, although there are no values reported for Qatar. We have designated a priority level of 1 or 2 for the indicators in the family life domain. Those with the lower priority ranking will require additional effort to calculate, such as those that require determining an official poverty line (which does not currently exist in Qatar) or other distributional measures (e.g., for consumption or income).

## *Education (ED-series)*

The education domain (coded ED-xxx) covers measures of illiteracy, school enrollment, educational attainment, training, educational expenditures, and educational services and infrastructure. Most of these indicators are currently in the prototype database, while others have been added as recommended by the QSCFA (e.g., students abroad at various levels [ED-008, ED-011, and ED-013], education expenditures per pupil [ED-033], fellowships for higher education [ED-034], expenditures related to research and development [R&D] [ED-035 to ED-037], counts of public and private schools [ED-039 and ED-040], vocational training centers [ED-043], and the teacher-to-pupil ratio at various levels [ED-048]). Among the additions we feature, we recommend the inclusion of net enrollment rates (ED-004) at each level (in addition to gross enrollment rates), measures of the distribution of the population by schooling level (ED-018 to ED-020), and rates of grade repetition (ED-022). Many of the population-based indicators would be calculated for subgroups, such as those defined by sex, age, nationality, and so on.

These various education indicators will be of particular interest to the Departments of Family, Childhood, Youth, and Special Needs. Most of the indicators that pertain to enrollment and education infrastructure are expected to come from the SEC, the Planning Council, or the Qatar Foundation, and will be available on an annual basis. Population-based data on illiteracy, enrollment rates, and educational attainment can be derived from the census and therefore are available less frequently. Nine indicators are included in the *Human Development Report* and values are available for Qatar in each case. We have assigned each indicator in the education domain one of the two highest priority rankings. Those rated as the highest priority capture key indicators that are readily available. Those with the next-highest priority are not as readily available.

## Health and Nutrition (HN-series)

The health and nutrition domain (coded HN-xxx) is one of the largest, with indicators that pertain to health and health services infrastructure, health services utilization in general and utilization of preventative services, health expenditures, nutritional status, women's reproductive health, health behaviors, domestic violence, disease incidence, and health services for those with special needs.[9] Most of these indicators are in the current prototype database. Several new indicators are included at the recommendation of the QSCFA (e.g., utilization of health care for acute conditions [HN-029], incidence of dental care [HN-033], various measures of per capita health care expenditures [HN-047 to HN-049], and drug-treatment rates [HN-070]). We recommend adding measures pertaining to full and partial immunization (HN-035, HN-037, HN-039, and HN-043), obesity (HN-051), contraceptive prevalence by method (HN-062), smoking prevalence (HN-068), domestic violence (HN-071), and several specific disease conditions (HN-090 to HN-096). We also indicate that drug-use prevalence rates (HN-069) should be calculated for the entire population and separately by age group. This will include the measure of youth drug use currently included in the prototype database.

Most indicators will be of interest to the Department of Family, while a subset will also be relevant for other departments such as those addressing women, childhood, the elderly, and those with special needs. These data will come from a variety of sources, including administrative data maintained by the MoH, NHA, HMC, and Planning Council, as well as data from vital statistics, the census, and specialized health surveys such as the FHS. As such, the frequency of the data will vary with the source, with most indicators available on an annual basis. In several cases, we indicate that new data collection is likely to be required in the form of a population-based survey or other source. A number of the measures

---

[9] Mortality indicators, which could also be covered here, are included in the population domain.

are included in the *Human Development Report,* but the indicators are not always reported for Qatar, indicating a possible lack of data.

We have assigned a priority of 1 or 2 to all but a few indicators. Those ranked somewhat lower-priority are indicators that are likely to be more difficult to obtain, given existing data sources. We also denote a few indicators as lower priority, level 3 or 4. These instances fall in the nutrition domain for indicators that will require new data collection in the form of a household nutrition survey. The incidence of nutrition problems such as undernourishment and child wasting and stunting are likely to be low in a high-income country like Qatar. Other lower-priority indicators relate to women's reproductive health, health behaviors, and disease conditions that would require new data collection or where the incidence is likely to be low. For example, two measures in the UNDP *Human Development Report* related to malaria incidence and treatment in children (namely children under age five infected with fever and treated with antimalarial drugs and children under age five sleeping under insecticide-treated bed nets) are likely to have very low incidence and are not currently reported for Qatar. We rate these measures as having the lowest priority.

## Environment (EV-series)

The environment domain (coded EV-xxx) features measures of the geography of the country and conditions of the air, water, and energy sector. With a few exceptions of new indicators suggested by the QSCFA (e.g., rate of land desertification [EV-002], water production [EV-007], and seashore pollution [EV-008]), the specific indicators are all currently included in the prototype database. These indicators are expected to be of greatest interest for the Department of Family, though other departments may find these measures useful as well.

Most of these measures, if they are currently available, are likely to come from specific ministries that focus on various aspects of the environment or possibly from the Planning Council. In most cases, they are likely to be available on an annual basis. Five of the indicators are included in the *Human Development Report,* although one indicator has no value for Qatar ("GDP per unit of energy usage"). We assign a rank of 2 or 3 to these indicators because they are less directly relevant to the QSCFA's current mission and goals, and most are not available from routine sources.

28

## Civil and Political Life (C-series)

The domain of civil and political life (coded C-xxx) encompasses indicators that pertain to cultural activities, athletic activities, and women's political participation. Generally, these are all indicators that are currently included in the prototype database. Several indicators are added based on the recommendations of the QSCFA (e.g., women's associations and unions [C-008], women's share as managers in public and private institutions [C-029]). A subset of the measures will be of greatest interest to the Department of Family, while others will be relevant for the activities of the Departments of Women, Youth, Childhood, and Special Needs.

These measures are likely to come from administrative data maintained by specific ministries or the private sector, as well as the annual statistical abstract produced by the Planning Council. In most cases, they would be available on an annual basis or possibly less frequently. With the exception of several of the indicators of women's political participation, these indicators are not included in the UNDP *Human Development Report*. We have given each indicator in this domain top priority, primarily because the data should be readily available.

## Safety and Security (SS-series)

The safety and security domain (coded SS-xxx) covers a diverse mix of indicators that address national security, crime, accidents, immigration, and refugees. A number of indicators (which are shown in italics) are not currently included in the prototype database and their addition is based on input from the QSCFA (e.g., measures of crime [SS-005 to SS-009] and accidents [S-010 to S-015]). Most measures will be of general interest to the Department of Family, and perhaps to others as well. Several others will have interest for almost every department. Some of the crime measures fall in to that category (e.g., the homicide rate).

In terms of data sources, these indicators are expected to come from specific ministries with these specific purviews, although we do not know for certain that all these indicators are currently available. In many cases, these indicators may be available on an annual basis, though some may not be produced as frequently. Some may require new data collection. Several of these indicators are included in the *Human Development Report* but they do not always have values for Qatar. The rankings of these indicators range from highest (1) to lowest (4). Those ranked highest are key indicators and standard measures that can be generated based on existing sources. Those with lowest priority, such as those pertaining to refugees, are less relevant for Qatar, in this case because Qatar does not send many refugees to other countries nor are there many refugees in Qatar. The two national security measures with a rank of 4 do not have values for Qatar in the *Human Development Report.*

## Statutory (ST-series)

The statutory domain (coded ST-xxx) differs from others in that it is not storing specific indicators but, rather, documents that pertain to specific conventions and treaties, including those pertaining to labor rights and the environment. These documents are likely to be of greatest interest to the Department of Family. However, several documents are specific to women, children, and those with special needs. Hence, as indicated in Table 3.2, they will be of interest for these departments as well. With one exception, they are all listed in the *Human Development Report* along with their current standings in Qatar. All of these documents are currently in the prototype database and hence they receive top priority ranking. Since these documents are a fixed resource, they will not need to be updated over time unless there is a change in the respective convention or treaty.

Table 3.2—Summary List of Indicators by Domain

Population

| Code / Indicator | Definition | Measurement Unit | Subgroups | | | | | | Departments | | | | | | Source Data | UNDP HDR | | Priority |
|---|---|---|---|---|---|---|---|---|---|---|---|---|---|---|---|---|---|---|
| | | | S | A | N | SN | H | G | F | W | C | Y | E | SN | | Indicator | Value (Y/N) | |
| **Population structure** | | | | | | | | | | | | | | | | | | |
| P-001 Total population | Total population or population in subgroups | Count | X | X | X | X | | X | X | X | X | X | X | X | Census | X | Y | 1 |
| P-002 *Total population distribution* | The ratio of the population in a subgroup divided by the total population | Percentage | X | X | X | X | | X | X | X | X | X | X | X | Census | | | 1 |
| P-003 Urban population | The ratio of population in urban areas divided by the total population | Percentage | | | | | | | X | X | X | X | X | X | Census | X | Y | 1 |
| P-004 *Dependency ratio* | Number of persons under age 15 or over age 64 divided by the number of persons age 15 to 64, multiplied by 100 | Ratio | | | | | | | X | X | X | X | X | X | Census, FHS | | | 1 |
| P-005 *Median age* | The age of the middle person in the age distribution; half the population will be younger than the median age, while half will be older | Value | | | | | | | X | X | X | X | X | X | Census | | | 1 |
| P-006 *Population density* | Total population in a given area divided by the square kilometers of that area | Persons per square km | | | | | | X | X | X | X | X | X | X | Census | | | 1 |
| P-007 Registered disabled persons | Number of disabled people who are registered at centers | Count | | | | | | | X | X | | | | X | Registries, PC | | | 1 |
| P-008 Self-reported disabled persons | Number of people who report they have a physical or mental limitation that limits participation in normal activities for a person their age | Count | | | | | | | X | X | | | | X | Census, FHS | | | 1 |
| **Population growth** | | | | | | | | | | | | | | | | | | |
| P-009 Annual population growth rate | Annual percentage change in population from one year to the next, or average annual percentage change in population over a period of years | Percentage | | | X | | | | X | X | | | | | Census | X | Y | 1 |
| P-010 Rate of natural increase | Birth rate (expressed as the number of births per 1,000 persons per year) minus the death rate (expressed as the number of deaths per 1,000 persons per year) | Per 1,000 persons | | | | | | | X | X | | | | | Census, VS | | | 1 |
| P-011 Registered live births | The number of live births recorded in vital statistics registries | Count | X | | X | | | | X | X | X | | | | VS | | | 1 |
| P-012 Crude birth rate | Annual number of births per 1,000 population | Per 1,000 persons | X | | X | | | | X | X | | X | | | Census, VS, FHS | | | 1 |
| P-013 *General birth rate* | Annual number of births per 1,000 women age 15–49 | Per 1,000 women | X | | X | | | | X | X | | X | | | Census, VS, FHS | | | 1 |
| P-014 Total fertility rate | The number of children that would be born to each woman if she were to live to the end of her childbearing years and bear children at each age in accordance with prevailing age-specific fertility rates | Value | X | | X | | | | X | X | | X | | | Census, VS, FHS | X | Y | 1 |

Table 3.2—Summary List of Indicators by Domain

| Code / Indicator | Definition | Measurement Unit | Subgroups | | | | | | Departments | | | | | | Source Data | UNDP HDR | | Priority |
|---|---|---|---|---|---|---|---|---|---|---|---|---|---|---|---|---|---|---|
| | | | S | A | N | SN | H | G | F | W | C | Y | E | SN | | Indicator | Value (Y/N) | |
| P-015 *Median age at first birth* | Among women age 15–49, median age at birth of first child | Value | X | X | X | | | | X | X | X | X | | | Census, VS, FHS | | | 1 |
| P-016 Crude death rate | Annual number of deaths per 1,000 population, or total number of deaths per year divided by total population | Per 1,000 persons | X | X | X | X | | | X | X | X | X | X | X | Census, VS | | | 1 |
| P-017 *Cause-specific mortality* | Annual number of deaths as a count or per 1,000 population from a specific cause (using ICD 10 or more detailed disaggregation), or total number of deaths per year from a specific cause as a count or divided by total population | Count, rate per 1,000 persons | X | X | X | X | | | X | X | X | X | X | X | VS | | | 1 |
| P-018 Infant mortality rate | The number of children in a birth cohort who die between birth and exactly 1 year of age divided by the number of births in the cohort, expressed per 1,000 live births | Per 1,000 live births | X | | X | | | | X | X | X | | | | VS, FHS | X | Y | 1 |
| P-019 Under age 5 child mortality rate | The number of children in a birth cohort who die between birth and exactly 5 years of age divided by the number of births in the cohort, expressed per 1,000 live births | Per 1,000 live births | X | | X | | | | X | X | X | | | | VS, FHS | X | Y | 1 |
| P-020 Maternal mortality ratio | The annual number of deaths of women from pregnancy-related causes divided by the number of births, expressed per 100,000 live births | Per 100,000 live births | | | | | | | X | X | X | | | | VS | X | Y | 1 |
| *Life expectancy* | | | | | | | | | | | | | | | | | | |
| P-021 Life expectancy at birth | The number of years a newborn infant would live if prevailing patterns of age-specific mortality rates at the time of birth were to stay the same throughout the child's lifetime | Years | X | | | | | | X | X | X | X | X | X | Census, VS | X | Y | 1 |
| P-022 Life expectancy index | A summary measure of the relative achievement of a country in life expectancy at birth (see UNDP, 2004, p. 259) | Value | | | | | | | X | X | X | X | X | | UNDP | X | Y | 1 |
| P-023 Survival rate to age 40 | The proportion of newborns who would be expected to live to age 40 if prevailing patterns of age-specific mortality rates at the time of birth were to stay the same throughout the child's lifetime | Percentage of cohort | X | | | | | | X | X | X | X | X | | Census, VS | X | Y | 1 |
| P-025 Survival rate to age 65 | The proportion of newborns who would be expected to live to age 65 if prevailing patterns of age-specific mortality rates at the time of birth were to stay the same throughout the child's lifetime | Percentage of cohort | X | | | | | | X | X | X | X | X | | Census, VS | X | Y | 1 |

**Table 3.2—Summary List of Indicators by Domain**

| Code / Indicator | Definition | Measurement Unit | Subgroups | | | | | | Departments | | | | | | Source Data | UNDP HDR | | Priority |
|---|---|---|---|---|---|---|---|---|---|---|---|---|---|---|---|---|---|---|
| | | | S | A | N | SN | H | G | F | W | C | Y | E | SN | | Indicator | Value (Y/N) | |
| **Economy** | | | | | | | | | | | | | | | | | | |
| *Overall economic activity* | | | | | | | | | | | | | | | | | | |
| E-001 GDP index | A summary measure of the size of a country's economy based on GDP per capita in PPP US$ (see UNDP, 2004, p. 259) | Value | | | | | | | X | | | | | | UNDP | X | Y | 1 |
| E-002 GDP | Gross domestic product, the sum of value added by all resident producers in the economy plus any product taxes not included in the valuation of output. | PPP US$, US$ | | | | | | | X | | | | | | National accounts | X | Y | 1 |
| E-003 GDP per capita | GDP divided by the total population | PPP US$, US$ | | | | | | | X | | | | | | National accounts | X | Y | 1 |
| E-005 GDP per capita annual growth rate | Annual percentage change in GDP from one year to the next or average annual percentage change in GDP over a period of years | Percentage | | | | | | | X | | | | | | National accounts | X | N | 1 |
| E-006 GDP per capita rank minus HDI rank | The difference in country rankings on GDP per capita index (PPP US$) and HDI (see UNDP, 2004, p. 259) | Value | | | | | | | X | | | | | | National accounts | X | Y | 1 |
| E-007 GDP per capita, highest value between years X and Y | The highest value in GDP per capita over a span of years (from year X to year Y) | PPP US$ | | | | | | | X | | | | | | National accounts | X | N | 1 |
| E-008 GDP per capita, year of highest value | The year GDP per capita reaches its highest value over a span of years (from year X to year Y) | Year | | | | | | | X | | | | | | National accounts | X | N | 1 |
| E-009 Gross national income | The sum of value added by all resident producers in the economy plus any product taxes (less subsidies) not included in the valuation of output plus net receipts of primary income (compensation of employees plus property income) from abroad | US$ | | | | | | | X | | | | | | National accounts | X | | 1 |
| E-010 Consumption GDP share | In national income accounts, the ratio of consumption to GDP | Percentage | | | | | | | X | | | | | | National accounts | | | 2 |
| E-011 Investment GDP share | In national income accounts, the ratio of investment to GDP | Percentage | | | | | | | X | | | | | | National accounts | | | 2 |
| E-012 Savings GDP share | In national income accounts, the ratio of savings to GDP | Percentage | | | | | | | X | | | | | | National accounts | | | 2 |
| E-013 Total debt services trade share | The sum of principal repayments and interest actually paid in foreign currency, goods, or services on long-term debt (a maturity of more than one year); interest paid on short-term debt; and repayments to the International Monetary Fund, as a share of the exports of goods and services | Percentage | | | | | | | X | | | | | | National accounts | X | N | 2 |
| E-014 Total debt service GDP share | The sum of principal repayments and interest actually paid in foreign currency, goods, or services on long-term debt (a maturity of more than one year); interest paid on short-term debt; and repayments to the International Monetary Fund, as a share of GDP | Percentage | | | | | | | X | | | | | | National accounts | X | N | 2 |

Table 3.2—Summary List of Indicators by Domain

| Code / Indicator | Definition | Measurement Unit | Subgroups | | | | | | Departments | | | | | | Source Data | UNDP HDR | | Priority |
|---|---|---|---|---|---|---|---|---|---|---|---|---|---|---|---|---|---|---|
| | | | S | A | N | SN | H | G | F | W | C | Y | E | SN | | Indicator | Value (Y/N) | |
| E-015 Net foreign direct investment inflows GDP share | Net inflows of investment to acquire a lasting management interest (10% or more of voting stock) in an enterprise operating in an economy other than that of the investor, divided by GDP | Percentage | | | | | | | X | | | | | | National accounts | X | N | 2 |
| E-016 Other private flows GDP share | Non-debt-creating portfolio equity investment flows, portfolio debt flows, and bank and trade-related lending | Percentage | | | | | | | X | | | | | | National accounts | X | N | 2 |
| E-017 GDP implicit price deflator | Current dollar GDP divided by constant dollar GDP, a measure of the rate of inflation reflected in the change in the prices of the bundle of goods and services that make up the GDP as well as changes in the bundle itself | Value | | | | | | | X | | | | | | National accounts | | | 1 |
| E-018 Level of the Consumer Price Index (CPI) | Price index measuring the cost to the average consumer of acquiring a basket of goods and services that may be fixed or may change at specified intervals | Value | | | | | | | X | | | | | | HEIS, PC | X | Y | 1 |
| E-019 Annual inflation rate (CPI-linked) | Change in the cost to the average consumer of acquiring a basket of goods and services that may be fixed or may change at specified intervals, measured by the annual rate of change in the level of the Consumer Price Index | Percentage | | | | | | | X | | | | | | HEIS, PC | X | Y | 1 |
| International trade | | | | | | | | | | | | | | | | | | |
| E-020 Imports of goods and services GDP share | The value of all goods and other market services received from the rest of the world divided by GDP | Percentage | | | | | | | X | | | | | | National accounts | X | N | 2 |
| E-021 Exports of goods and services GDP share | The value of all goods and other market services provided to the rest of the world divided by GDP | Percentage | | | | | | | X | | | | | | National accounts | X | N | 2 |
| E-022 Primary exports share | Exports of food, agricultural raw materials, fuels and ores, and metals divided by merchandise exports | Percentage | | | | | | | X | | | | | | National accounts | X | Y | 2 |
| E-023 Manufactured exports share | Exports of chemicals, basic manufactures, machinery, transport equipment, and other miscellaneous manufacturer goods divided by merchandise exports | Percentage | | | | | | | X | | | | | | National accounts | X | Y | 2 |
| E-024 High-technology exports share | Exports of products with a high intensity of research and development divided by merchandise exports | Percentage | | | | | | | X | | | | | | National accounts | X | Y | 2 |
| E-025 Terms of trade | Ratio of the export price index to the import price index measured relative to a base year | Percentage | | | | | | | X | | | | | | National accounts | X | N | 2 |

Table 3.2—Summary List of Indicators by Domain

| Code / Indicator | Definition | Measurement Unit | Subgroups | | | | | | Departments | | | | | | Source Data | UNDP HDR Indicator | UNDP HDR Value (Y/N) | Priority |
|---|---|---|---|---|---|---|---|---|---|---|---|---|---|---|---|---|---|---|
| | | | S | A | N | SN | H | G | F | W | C | Y | E | SN | | | | |
| **Human development indicators** | | | | | | | | | | | | | | | | | | |
| E-026 Human development index (HDI) | A summary measure of human development derived by the UNDP: an average of the life expectancy index, the education index, and the GDP index (see UNDP, 2004, p. 259) | Value, rank | | | | | | | X | X | X | | | | UNDP | X | Y | 1 |
| E-027 Gender-related development index (GDI) | A summary measure of gender inequality derived by the UNDP based on differences between in men and women in life expectancy, adult literacy and school enrollment rates, and earned income (see UNDP, 2004, pp. 261–262) | Value, rank | | | | | | | X | X | | X | | | UNDP | X | N | 2 |
| E-028 Gender-empowerment measure (GEM) | A summary measure of gender inequality derived by the UNDP based on differences between men and women in political participation, economic participation, and power over economic resources (see UNDP, 2004, p. 263) | Value, rank | | | | | | | X | X | | X | | | UNDP | X | N | 2 |
| E-029 HDI rank minus GDI rank | The difference in country rankings on the HDI and GDI (see UNDP, 2004, pp. 259, 261–262) | Difference in ranks | | | | | | | X | X | X | | | | UNDP | X | N | 2 |
| **Development assistance** | | | | | | | | | | | | | | | | | | |
| E-030 Total net Official Development Assistance (ODA) received | Disbursements of loans made on concessional terms (net of repayments of principal) and grants by official agencies to promote economic development | US$ millions | | | | | | | X | | | | | | National accounts | X | Y | 2 |
| E-031 Net ODA received per capita | ODA divided by the total population | US$ | | | | | | | X | | | | | | National accounts | X | Y | 2 |
| E-032 Net ODA received GDP share | ODA divided by GDP | Percentage | | | | | | | X | | | | | | National accounts | X | N | 2 |
| **Technology** | | | | | | | | | | | | | | | | | | |
| E-033 Telephone mainlines and cellular subscribers | Sum of telephone mainlines and cellular subscribers divided by total population | Per 100 persons | | | | | | | X | | | X | | | Public- and/or private-sector administrative data | X | Y | 1 |
| E-034 Telephone mainlines | Telephone lines connecting a customer's equipment to the public-switched telephone network, divided by the total population | Per 1,000 persons | | | | | | | X | | | X | | | Public- and/or private-sector administrative data | X | Y | 1 |
| E-035 Cellular subscribers | Subscribers to an automatic public mobile-telephone service that provides access to the public switched telephone network using cellular technology, either analog or digital, divided by the total population | Per 1,000 persons | | | | | | | X | | | X | | | Public- and/or private-sector administrative data | X | Y | 1 |
| E-037 Internet users | Number of people with access to the worldwide network divided by the total population | Per 1,000 persons | | | | | | | X | | | X | | | Public- and/or private-sector administrative data | X | Y | 1 |
| E-038 Personal computers | Number of personal computers divided by total population | Per 100 persons | | | | | | | X | | | X | | | Public- and/or private-sector administrative data | X | | 1 |

34

Table 3.2—Summary List of Indicators by Domain

| Code / Indicator | Definition | Measurement Unit | Subgroups | | | | | | Departments | | | | | | Source Data | UNDP HDR | | Priority |
|---|---|---|---|---|---|---|---|---|---|---|---|---|---|---|---|---|---|---|
| | | | S | A | N | SN | H | G | F | W | C | Y | E | SN | | Indicator | Value (Y/N) | |
| E-039 Radio access in households | Number of households with a radio divided by the total number of households | Percentage | | | | | | | X | | | X | | | Census or other population-based survey | | | 2 |
| E-040 TV access in households | Number of households with a television divided by the total number of households | Percentage | | | | | | | X | | | X | | | Census or other population-based survey | | | 2 |
| E-041 Fixed-line telephone access in households | Number of households with a fixed line telephone divided by the total number of households | Percentage | | | | | | | X | | | X | | | Census or other population-based survey | | | 2 |
| E-042 Cellular access in households | Number of households with a mobile cellular telephone divided by the total number of households | Percentage | | | | | | | X | | | X | | | Census or other population-based survey | | | 2 |
| E-043 Computers in use in households | Number of households with a computer divided by the total number of households | Percentage | | | | | | | X | | | X | | | Census or other population-based survey | | | 2 |
| E-044 Internet access in households | Number of households with Internet access divided by the total number of households | Percentage | | | | | | | X | | | X | | | Census or other population-based survey | | | 2 |
| E-045 Business computer use | Number of businesses using computers divided by the total number of businesses | Percentage | | | | | | | X | | | X | | | Business survey or census | | | 1 |
| E-046 Business Internet use | Number of businesses using the Internet divided by the total number of businesses | Percentage | | | | | | | X | | | X | | | Business survey or census | | | 1 |
| E-047 Employee computer use | Number of employees using computers divided by the total number of employees | Percentage | | | | | | | X | | | X | | | Labor force or other population-based survey | | | 1 |
| E-048 Employee Internet use | Number of employees using the Internet divided by the total number of employees | Percentage | | | | | | | X | | | X | | | Labor force or other population-based survey | | | 1 |
| E-049 Patents granted to residents | Documents issued by a government office that describe an invention and create a legal situation in which the patented invention can normally be exploited only by or with the authorization of the patentee, divided by the total population | Per million people | | | | | | | X | | | | | | Public- and/or private-sector administrative data | X | N | 2 |
| E-050 Receipts of royalties and license fees | Receipts by residents from non-residents for the authorized use of intangible, non-produced, non-financial assets and proprietary rights and for the use of produced originals of prototypes, divided by the total population | US$ per person | | | | | | | X | | | | | | Public- and/or private-sector administrative data | X | N | 2 |
| E-051 Expenditure on research and development (R&D) GDP share | Current and capital expenditures on creative, systematic activity intended to increase the stock of knowledge, divided by the total population or by GDP | Per million persons, percentage | | | | | | | X | | | | | | Public- and/or private-sector administrative data | X | N | 2 |

**Table 3.2—Summary List of Indicators by Domain**

| Code / Indicator | Definition | Measurement Unit | Subgroups | | | | | | Departments | | | | | | Source Data | UNDP HDR | | Priority |
|---|---|---|---|---|---|---|---|---|---|---|---|---|---|---|---|---|---|---|
| | | | S | A | N | SN | H | G | F | W | C | Y | E | SN | | Indicator | Value (Y/N) | |
| **Labor force** | | | | | | | | | | | | | | | | | | |
| E-052 *Economically active population* | The number of persons in total (or in a subgroup) who supply, or are available to supply, labor for the production of goods and services | Count | X | X | X | X | X | X | X | X | X | X | X | X | LFS | | | 1 |
| E-053 *Rate of economic activity among the population* | The number of persons in total (or in a subgroup) who supply, or are available to supply, labor for the production of goods and services, divided by the total (or subgroup) population | Percentage | X | X | X | X | X | X | X | X | X | X | X | X | LFS | X | Y | 1 |
| E-054 *Annual growth rate of the labor force* | Annual percentage change in GDP from one year to the next or average annual percentage change in GDP over a period of years | Percentage | | | | | | | X | | | | | | Census, LFS | | | 1 |
| E-055 *Retired population* | Number of persons in total (or in a subgroup) who report they are not working and are retired | Count | X | X | X | | | | X | X | | | X | | LFS | | | 1 |
| E-056 *Retirement rate* | Number of persons in total (or in a subgroup) who report they are not working and are retired divided by the total (or subgroup) population | Percentage | X | X | X | | | | X | X | | | X | | LFS | | | 1 |
| **Employment** | | | | | | | | | | | | | | | | | | |
| E-057 *Population employed* | The number of persons in total (or in a subgroup) who are with a job at work or temporarily absent from a job | Count | X | X | X | X | X | X | X | X | X | X | X | X | LFS | | | 1 |
| E-058 *Employment rate* | The number of persons in total (or in a subgroup) who are with a job at work or temporarily absent from a job divided by the total (or subgroup) population | Percentage | X | X | X | X | X | X | X | X | X | X | X | X | LFS | | | 1 |
| E-059 *Employment by sector* | The number who are employed in jobs in the public or private sector | Count | X | X | | | | | X | X | | X | X | | LFS | | | 1 |
| E-060 *Employment by class* | The number who are employed in jobs defined by whether they are paid employees or self-employed | Count | X | X | | | | | X | X | | X | X | | LFS | | | 1 |
| E-061 *Employment by industry* | The number who are employed in different industries | Count | X | X | | | | | X | X | | X | X | | LFS | X | N | 1 |
| E-062 *Employment by occupation* | The number who are employed in different occupations | Count | X | X | | | | | X | X | | X | X | | LFS | | | 1 |
| E-063 *Distribution of employment by sector* | The number who are employed in jobs in the public or private sector divided by total employment | Percentage | X | X | | | | | X | X | | X | X | | LFS | | | 1 |
| E-064 *Distribution of employment by class* | The number who are employed in jobs defined by whether they are paid employees or self-employed divided by total employment | Percentage | X | X | | | | | X | X | | X | X | | LFS | | | 1 |
| E-065 *Distribution of employment by industry* | The number who are employed in different industries divided by total employment | Percentage | X | | | | | | X | X | | X | X | | LFS | | | 1 |
| E-066 *Distribution of employment by occupation* | The number who are employed in different occupations divided by total employment | Percentage | X | | | | | | X | X | | X | X | | LFS | | | 1 |
| E-067 *Average usual hours of work* | Average hours worked by employed workers in a typical week (usual hours) | Value | X | X | | | | | X | X | | X | X | | LFS | | | 1 |
| E-068 *Average actual and overtime hours of work* | Average actual and overtime hours worked by employed workers in the reference week | Value | X | X | | | | | X | X | | X | X | | LFS | | | 1 |
| E-069 *Average monthly salary* | Average monthly salary for employed workers | Value | X | X | | | | | X | X | | X | X | | LFS | | | 1 |

36

Table 3.2—Summary List of Indicators by Domain

| Code / Indicator | Definition | Measurement Unit | Subgroups | | | | | | Departments | | | | | | Source Data | UNDP HDR | | Priority |
|---|---|---|---|---|---|---|---|---|---|---|---|---|---|---|---|---|---|---|
| | | | S | A | N | SN | H | G | F | W | C | Y | E | SN | | Indicator | Value (Y/N) | |
| **Unemployment** | | | | | | | | | | | | | | | | | | |
| E-070 *Population unemployed* | The number of persons in total (or in a subgroup) who are not with a job or temporarily absent from a job, but are available to look and actively looking for work | Count | X | X | X | X | X | X | X | X | | X | X | X | LFS | | | 1 |
| E-071 Unemployment rate | The number of persons in total (or in a subgroup) who are not with a job or temporarily absent from a job, but are available to look and actively looking for work, divided by the total (or subgroup) population | Percentage | X | X | X | X | X | X | X | X | | X | X | X | LFS | X | N | 1 |
| E-072 Unemployed who have never been employed before | The number of unemployed who report they have never been employed before (new entrants) divided by the number of unemployed | Percentage | X | X | | | | | X | X | | X | | | LFS | | | 1 |
| E-073 Unemployed who have been employed before | The number of unemployed who report they have been employed before (reentrants) divided by the number of unemployed | Percentage | X | X | | | | | X | X | | X | | | LFS | | | 1 |
| E-074 *Population of discouraged workers* | The number of persons who are able and willing to work but who are not actively looking for work (counted as not in the labor force above) | Count | X | X | | X | | | X | X | | X | | X | LFS | | | 1 |
| E-075 *Incidence of discouraged workers* | The number of persons in total (or in a subgroup) who are able and willing to work but who are not actively looking for work (counted as not in the labor force above), divided by the total (or subgroup) population | Percentage | X | X | | X | | | X | X | | X | | X | LFS | | | 1 |

Table 3.2—Summary List of Indicators by Domain

| Code / Indicator | Definition | Measurement Unit | Subgroups | | | | | | Departments | | | | | | Source Data | UNDP HDR Indicator | UNDP HDR Value (Y/N) | Priority |
|---|---|---|---|---|---|---|---|---|---|---|---|---|---|---|---|---|---|---|
| | | | S | A | N | SN | H | G | F | W | C | Y | E | SN | | | | |
| **Family Life** | | | | | | | | | | | | | | | | | | |
| **Household structure and composition** | | | | | | | | | | | | | | | | | | |
| F-001 *Total number of households* | Count of households | Count | | | | | X | | X | X | X | X | X | | Census, FHS, HEIS | | | 1 |
| F-002 Total household distribution | Number of households of different types divided by the total number of households | Percentage | | | | | X | | X | X | X | X | X | | Census, FHS, HEIS | | | 1 |
| F-003 Average household size | Average number of persons in households | Value | | | | | X | | X | X | X | X | X | | Census, FHS, HEIS | | | 1 |
| F-004 *Orphaned children* | Count of number of orphaned children | Count | X | X | | | | | X | X | X | X | X | | Census or registries | | | 1 |
| **Marriage and divorce** | | | | | | | | | | | | | | | | | | |
| F-005 Crude marriage rate | Total number of registered marriages in a year divided by total population | Per 100,000 persons | X | X | | | | | X | X | X | X | | | VS | | | 1 |
| F-006 Crude divorce rate | Total number of registered divorces in a year divided by total population | Per 100,000 persons | X | X | | | | | X | X | X | X | | | VS | | | 1 |
| F-007 Average age at time of first marriage | Mean age at first marriage among those who marry by age 50 (also known as the singulate mean age at marriage) | Years | X | | | | | | X | X | X | X | | | FHS | | | 1 |
| F-008 Population who are never married | Number of persons above a given age who are never married, count or divided by the total population in the age group | Count, percentage | X | X | X | X | | | X | X | X | X | X | | Census, FHS, HEIS, LFS | | | 1 |
| F-009 Population who are married | Number of persons above a given age who are currently married, count or divided by the total population in the age group | Count, percentage | X | X | X | X | | | X | X | X | X | X | | Census, FHS, HEIS, LFS | | | 1 |
| F-010 *Population who are in polygamous marriages* | Number of persons above a given age who are currently in a polygamous marriage, count or divided by the total population in the age group | Count, percentage | X | X | X | X | | | X | X | X | X | X | | Census, FHS | | | 1 |
| F-011 Population who are separated | Number of persons above a given age who are currently separated, count or divided by the total population in the age group | Count, percentage | X | X | X | X | | | X | X | X | X | X | | Census, FHS, HEIS, LFS | | | 1 |
| F-012 Population who are divorced | Number of persons above a given age who are currently divorced, count or divided by the total population in the age group | Count, percentage | X | X | X | X | | | X | X | X | X | X | | Census, FHS, HEIS, LFS | | | 1 |
| F-013 Population who are widowed | Number of persons above a given age who are currently widowed, count or divided by the total population in the age group | Count, percentage | X | X | X | X | | | X | X | X | X | X | | Census, FHS, HEIS, LFS | | | 1 |

**Table 3.2—Summary List of Indicators by Domain**

| Code / Indicator | Definition | Measurement Unit | Subgroups S | A | N | SN | H | G | Departments F | W | C | Y | E | SN | Source Data | UNDP HDR Indicator | Value (Y/N) | Priority |
|---|---|---|---|---|---|---|---|---|---|---|---|---|---|---|---|---|---|---|
| **Housing characteristics** | | | | | | | | | | | | | | | | | | |
| F-014 *Distribution of households by tenure (rent, own)* | Number of households that rent or own their homes, divided by the total number of households | Percentage | | | X | | X | X | X | X | X | X | X | | Census | | | 1 |
| F-015 Residential buildings that are connected to the general water grid | Number of residential buildings connected to the general water grid, divided by the total number of residential buildings | Percentage | | | | | | X | X | | | | | | Census | | | 1 |
| F-016 Residential buildings that are connected to the sewage system networks | Number of residential buildings connected to the sewage system, divided by the total number of residential buildings | Percentage | | | | | | X | X | | | | | | Census | | | 1 |
| F-017 Residential buildings that are connected to the public electricity network | Number of residential buildings connected to the public electricity network, divided by the total number of residential buildings | Percentage | | | | | | X | X | | | | | | Census | | | 1 |
| F-018 Subsisting households that have a bathroom inside the house | Number of subsistence households with a bathroom inside the house, divided by the total number of subsidence households | Percentage | | | | | | X | X | | | | | | Census | | | 1 |
| F-019 Subsisting households that use gas in the kitchen | Number of subsistence households that use gas inside the kitchen, divided by the total number of subsidence households | Percentage | | | | | | X | X | | | | | | Census | | | 1 |
| **Poverty** | | | | | | | | | | | | | | | | | | |
| F-020 Population living below the national poverty line | Number of people with household income below the national poverty line, divided by the total population | Count, percentage | X | X | X | X | X | X | X | X | X | X | X | X | HEIS | X | N | 1 |
| F-021 Poverty gap ratio | Mean percentage distance between actual income and poverty line for households that are classified as poor | Percentage | | | | | | | X | X | | | | | HEIS | | | 2 |
| F-022 *Human Poverty Index (HPI-2)* | A summary measure of poverty for developed countries derived by the UNDP based on the survival rate (to age 60), the adult illiteracy rate, the percentage of people living below 50% of median-adjusted household disposable income, and rate of long-term (12 months or more) unemployment (see UNDP, 2004, p. 260) | Rank, value | | | | | | | X | X | | | | | PC, HEIS, LFS | X | N | 2 |

Table 3.2—Summary List of Indicators by Domain

| Code / Indicator | Definition | Measurement Unit | S | A | N | SN | H | G | F | W | C | Y | E | SN | Source Data | Indicator | Value (Y/N) | Priority |
|---|---|---|---|---|---|---|---|---|---|---|---|---|---|---|---|---|---|---|
| **Income** | | | | | | | | | | | | | | | | | | |
| F-023 Female estimated earned income | Estimate of earned income per woman (in PPP US $) calculated from the ratio of female nonagricultural wage to the male nonagricultural wage, female share of the economically active population, total female population, and GDP per capita (in PPP US$) (see UNDP, 2004, p. 264) | PPP US$ | | | | | | | X | X | | | | | Census, LFS, national accounts | X | N | 2 |
| F-024 Male estimated earned income | Estimate of earned income per man (in PPP US $) calculated from the ratio of female nonagricultural wage to the male nonagricultural wage, male share of the economically active population, total male population, and GDP per capita (in PPP US$) (see UNDP, 2004, p. 264) | PPP US$ | | | | | | | X | X | | | | | Census, LFS, national accounts | X | N | 2 |
| F-025 Female earned income relative to male earned income | Ratio of estimated female earned income to estimated male earned income (see UNDP, 2004, p. 264) | Ratio | | | | | | | X | X | | | | | HEIS | X | N | 2 |
| F-026 Share of income or consumption—Poorest 10% | Share of total income or total consumption that is earned by the poorest 10 percent of families or persons. | Percentage | | | | | | | X | X | | | | | HEIS | X | N | 2 |
| F-027 Share of income or consumption—Poorest 20% | Share of total income or total consumption that is earned by the poorest 20 percent of families or persons | Percentage | | | | | | | X | X | | | | | HEIS | X | N | 2 |
| F-028 Share of income or consumption—Richest 10% | Share of total income or total consumption that is earned by the richest 10 percent of families or persons | Percentage | | | | | | | X | X | | | | | HEIS | X | N | 2 |
| F-029 Share of income or consumption—Richest 20% | Share of total income or total consumption that is earned by the richest 20 percent of families or persons | Percentage | | | | | | | X | X | | | | | HEIS | X | N | 2 |
| F-030 Ratio of richest 10% to poorest 10% | Ratio of income at the 10th percentile of the income or consumption distribution to the 90th percentile | Ratio | | | | | | | X | X | | | | | HEIS | X | N | 2 |
| F-031 Ratio of richest 20% to poorest 20% | Ratio of income at the 20th percentile of the income or consumption distribution to the 80th percentile | Ratio | | | | | | | X | X | | | | | HEIS | X | N | 2 |
| F-032 Gini index | A summary measure of dispersion in the distribution of income or consumption; a value of zero represents percent equality; a value of 100 represents perfect inequality (see Lerman and Yitzhaki, 1984) | Value | | | | | | | X | X | | | | | HEIS | X | N | 2 |
| F-033 Share of household income from female earnings | Average across households of the ratio of female earnings to total household earnings | Percentage | | | | | | | X | X | | | | | HEIS | | | 2 |
| F-034 Share of household income from male earnings | Average across households of the ratio of male earnings to total household earnings | Percentage | | | | | | | X | X | | | | | HEIS | | | 2 |
| F-035 Average household monthly income | Average across all households of monthly income | US$ | | | X | | X | X | X | X | | | | | HEIS | | | 1 |
| F-036 Average household monthly income of persons | Average monthly household income for persons in the population | US$ | | | X | X | X | X | X | X | | | | | HEIS | | | 1 |
| F-037 Percentage of the population who do not have any source of living | Number of people with no recorded source of income or inkind benefits, divided by total population | Percentage | X | X | X | | | | X | X | | | X | | HEIS | | | 2 |
| F-038 *Average household debt* | Average across households in the level of debt | US$ | | | | | | | X | X | | | X | | *New data collection* | | | 2 |

40

**Table 3.2—Summary List of Indicators by Domain**

| Code / Indicator | Definition | Measurement Unit | Subgroups |  |  |  |  |  | Departments |  |  |  |  |  | Source Data | UNDP HDR |  | Priority |
|---|---|---|---|---|---|---|---|---|---|---|---|---|---|---|---|---|---|---|
|  |  |  | S | A | N | SN | H | G | F | W | C | Y | E | SN |  | Indicator | Value (Y/N) |  |
| **Consumption** |  |  |  |  |  |  |  |  |  |  |  |  |  |  |  |  |  |  |
| F-039 Average monthly household consumption | Average monthly spending by households on goods and services | Value |  |  |  |  |  |  | X | X |  |  | X |  | *HEIS* |  |  | 2 |
| F-040 Average monthly per capita household consumption | Average of monthly per capita (per person in the household) household spending on goods and services | Value |  |  |  |  |  |  | X | X |  |  | X |  | HEIS |  |  | 1 |
| F-041 Household consumer units | Number of households according to survey on household consumption | Value |  |  |  |  |  |  | X | X |  |  | X |  | HEIS |  |  | 1 |
| **Social support** |  |  |  |  |  |  |  |  |  |  |  |  |  |  |  |  |  |  |
| F-042 *Beneficiaries of Zakat* | Number of individuals receiving Zakat (obligatory charitable duty) or as a share of total population | *Count, percentage* | X |  |  |  |  |  | X | X |  |  |  |  | *HEIS* |  |  | 2 |
| F-043 Beneficiaries of private or public financial aid | Number of individuals receiving private or public financial assistance or as a share of total population | *Count, percentage* | X |  |  |  |  |  | X | X |  |  |  |  | *HEIS* |  |  | 2 |
| F-044 Beneficiaries of social security | Number of individuals receiving social security or as a share of total population | *Count, percentage* | X |  |  |  |  |  | X | X |  |  | X |  | *HEIS, administrative records* |  |  | 2 |
| F-045 Elderly in care centers | Number of elderly in care centers | *Count, percentage* |  |  |  |  |  |  | X |  |  |  | X |  | *Administrative records* |  |  | 2 |
| F-046 Beneficiaries of population-support | Number of individuals receiving population-support or as a share of total population | *Count, percentage* |  |  |  |  |  |  | X |  |  |  | X |  | *HEIS* |  |  | 2 |
| F-047 Population who benefit from health insurance | Number of individuals with health insurance coverage | *Count, percentage* |  |  |  |  |  |  | X |  |  |  | X |  | *NHA, HMC* |  |  | 2 |
| F-048 Beneficiaries of pensions | Number of individuals receiving pensions or as a share of total population | *Count, percentage* |  |  |  |  |  |  | X |  |  |  | X |  | *HEIS* |  |  | 2 |

Table 3.2—Summary List of Indicators by Domain

| Code / Indicator | Definition | Measurement Unit | Subgroups | | | | | | Departments | | | | | | Source Data | UNDP HDR | | Priority |
|---|---|---|---|---|---|---|---|---|---|---|---|---|---|---|---|---|---|---|
| | | | S | A | N | SN | H | G | F | W | C | Y | E | SN | | Indicator | Value (Y/N) | |
| **Education** | | | | | | | | | | | | | | | | | | |
| **Illiteracy** | | | | | | | | | | | | | | | | | | |
| ED-001 Illiteracy rate | Percentage of the population age 15 and above who can, with understanding, both read and write a short, simple statement related to their everyday life | Percentage | X | X | X | X | | X | X | X | X | X | X | X | Census, FHS | X | Y | 1 |
| **Education enrollment** | | | | | | | | | | | | | | | | | | |
| ED-002 Enrollment in early-childhood education or early-childhood development programs | Number of children attending some form of organized early-childhood education or early-childhood development program, or as a share of population of children not yet enrolled in kindergarten | *Count, percentage* | X | X | X | X | | | X | | | | | X | *Census, SEC* | | | 2 |
| ED-003 Gross enrollment rates at the primary, secondary, and higher-education levels | The number of students enrolled at a given level of education, regardless of age, as a percentage of the population of official school age for that level (this rate can be greater than 100) | Percentage | X | X | X | X | | | X | | X | X | | X | Census, SEC | | | 1 |
| ED-004 *Net enrollment rates at the primary, secondary, and higher-education levels* | The number of students enrolled at a given level of education who are of official school age for that level, as a percentage of the population of official school age for that level | Percentage | X | X | X | X | | | X | | X | X | | X | Census, SEC | X | Y | 1 |
| ED-005 Orphan to non-orphan school enrollment rates | Ratio of enrollment rate for orphans to the enrollment rate of non-orphans by level of schooling | Percentage | | | | | | | X | | X | X | | X | *Registries, SEC* | | | 2 |
| ED-006 Students in private K-12 schools | Number of students enrolled in private K-12 schools | Count | X | X | X | X | | | X | | X | X | | X | PC, SEC | | | 1 |
| ED-007 Students in public K-12 schools | Number of students enrolled in public K-12 schools | Count | X | X | X | X | | | X | | X | X | | X | PC, SEC | | | 1 |
| ED-008 *Students abroad in K-12 schools* | Number of students enrolled in K-12 schools abroad sponsored (paid for) by their families | Count | X | X | X | X | | | X | | X | X | | X | *PC, SEC* | | | 1 |
| ED-009 Students in universities | Number of students enrolled in universities | Count | X | X | X | X | | | X | | X | X | | X | PC, SEC | | | 1 |
| ED-010 Students abroad in college on scholarship | Number of students on study-abroad scholarships to obtain university degrees | Count | X | X | X | X | | | X | | | X | | X | PC, SEC | | | 1 |
| ED-011 *Students abroad in college on family support* | Number of students studying abroad to obtain university degrees sponsored (paid for) by their families | Count | X | X | X | X | | | X | | X | X | | X | *PC, SEC* | | | 1 |
| ED-012 Students in post-graduate studies | Number of students enrolled in post-graduate studies | Count | X | X | X | X | | | X | | | X | | X | PC, SEC | | | 1 |
| ED-013 *Students abroad in post-graduate studies* | Number of students on study-abroad scholarships to obtain post-graduate degrees | Count | X | X | X | X | | | X | | | X | | X | PC, SEC | | | 1 |
| ED-014 Students in special education schools | Number of students enrolled in special education schools | Count | X | X | X | X | | | X | | X | X | | X | PC, SEC | | | 1 |
| ED-015 Students in Al-Noor Institute | Number of students enrolled in Al-Noor Institute | Count | X | X | | X | | | X | | X | X | | X | PC, SEC | | | 1 |
| ED-016 Students in adult literacy centers and night schools | Number of students enrolled in adult literacy centers and night schools | Count | X | X | | | | | X | | | | | | PC, SEC | | | 1 |
| ED-017 Students age 65+ in adult literacy centers and night schools | Number of students age 65+ enrolled in adult literacy centers and night schools | Count | X | X | | X | | | X | | | | X | | PC, SEC | | | 1 |

Table 3.2—Summary List of Indicators by Domain

| Code / Indicator | Definition | Measurement Unit | Subgroups S | A | N | SN | H | G | Departments F | W | C | Y | E | SN | Source Data | UNDP HDR Indicator | Value (Y/N) | Priority |
|---|---|---|---|---|---|---|---|---|---|---|---|---|---|---|---|---|---|---|
| **Educational attainment** | | | | | | | | | | | | | | | | | | |
| ED-018 *Educational attainment of the population by years or level* | Number and share of population with educational attainment at each of several specified levels | Count, percentage | X | X | X | X | X | X | X | X | X | X | X | X | Census, FHS | | | 1 |
| ED-019 *High school graduates* | Number and share of population with high school diploma | Count, percentage | X | | X | X | | | X | X | X | X | | X | Census, SEC | | | 1 |
| ED-020 *University graduates* | Number and share of population with 4-year diploma | Count, percentage | X | | X | X | | | X | X | X | X | | X | Census, SEC | | | 1 |
| ED-021 Children who reach grade 5 | The number of children starting primary school who eventually attain grade 5, divided by the size of the cohort starting primary school | Percentage | X | | X | X | | | X | X | X | | | X | SEC | X | Y | 2 |
| ED-022 *Rate of grade repetition* | Number of students in a specified grade (schooling level) who repeat that grade (level), divided by the number of students in the grade (level) | Percentage | X | X | | | | | | | | | | | SEC | | | 2 |
| ED-023 Failure rate in secondary education | Number of individuals who started secondary education but did not finish, divided by the population that started the education level | Percentage | X | | X | X | | | X | X | X | X | | X | SEC | | | 2 |
| ED-024 Benefit rate from the merger project for the disabled | Percentage of disabled people who benefit from the merger project | Percentage | | | | | | | | | | | | X | SEC | | | 2 |
| **Training** | | | | | | | | | | | | | | | | | | |
| ED-025 Trainees in the Institute of Administrative Development | Number of trainees in the Institute of Administrative Development | Count | X | X | | | | | X | X | | X | | X | SEC | | | 2 |
| ED-026 Trainees in the Languages Center | Number of trainees in the Languages Center | Count | X | X | | | | | X | X | | | | | SEC | | | 2 |
| ED-027 Students enrolled in vocational training centers | Number of students enrolled in vocational training centers | Count | X | X | | | | | X | X | | X | | | SEC | | | 1 |

43

Table 3.2—Summary List of Indicators by Domain

| Code / Indicator | Definition | Measurement Unit | Subgroups | | | | | | Departments | | | | | | Source Data | UNDP HDR | | Priority |
|---|---|---|---|---|---|---|---|---|---|---|---|---|---|---|---|---|---|---|
| | | | S | A | N | SN | H | G | F | W | C | Y | E | SN | | Indicator | Value (Y/N) | |
| **Education expenditures and financing** | | | | | | | | | | | | | | | | | | |
| ED-028 Public expenditure on pre-primary and primary education | Public education expenditures (capital expenditures and current expenditures) on pre-primary and primary education divided by total public education expenditures | US$ million, *percentage* | | | | | | | X | X | X | X | | | *SEC* | X | Y | 1 |
| ED-029 Public expenditure on secondary education | Public education expenditures (capital expenditures and current expenditures) on secondary education divided by total public education expenditures | US$ million, *percentage* | | | | | | | X | X | X | X | | | *SEC* | X | Y | 1 |
| ED-030 Public expenditure on tertiary education | Public education expenditures (capital expenditures and current expenditures) on tertiary education divided by total public education expenditures | US$ million, *percentage* | | | | | | | X | X | X | X | | | *SEC* | X | Y | 1 |
| ED-031 Public expenditure on education as share of GDP | Total public education expenditures (capital expenditures and current expenditures) divided by GDP | US$ million, *percentage* | | | | | | | X | X | X | X | | | *SEC, national accounts* | X | Y | 1 |
| ED-032 Share of government spending on public education | Total public education expenditures (capital expenditures and current expenditures) divided by total government expenditures | US$ million, *percentage* | | | | | | | X | X | X | X | | | *SEC, national accounts* | X | Y | 1 |
| ED-033 *Education expenditures per pupil, total and by type* | Public and private education expenditures (capital expenditures and current expenditures) at all levels, in total and for private education and for education abroad, all divided by number of students in each type of education (total, private, abroad) | QR decomposition per capita | | | | | | | X | X | X | X | | | *SEC, private schools* | | | 1 |
| ED-034 *Fellowships for higher education by level and specialty* | Number of fellowships for higher education by level and specialty | Count | X | | | | | | X | X | X | X | | | *SEC* | | | 2 |
| *Education expenditures on R&D* | | | | | | | | | | | | | | | | | | |
| ED-035 *Share of education expenditure for R&D* | Total education expenditures on scientific research and technical development, divided by total education expenditures | Percentage | | | | | | | X | X | X | X | | | *PC, SEC, QF* | | | 2 |
| ED-036 *Share of education expenditure for data and networking* | Total education expenditures on statistical data collection, analyses, and setting up of electronic networks, divided by total education expenditures | Percentage | | | | | | | X | X | X | X | | | *PC, SEC, QF* | | | 2 |
| ED-037 *Education expenditure on R&D as a share of GDP* | Total education expenditures on scientific research and technical development divided by GDP | Percentage | | | | | | | X | X | X | X | | | *PC, SEC, QF* | | | 2 |
| Education index | | | | | | | | | | | | | | | | | | |
| ED-038 Education index | A summary measure of education derived by the UNDP based on the adult literacy rate, and the combined gross enrollment ratio for primary, secondary, and tertiary schools (see UNDP, 2004, p. 259) | Percentage | | | | | | | X | X | X | X | | | UNDP | X | Y | 1 |

44

Table 3.2—Summary List of Indicators by Domain

| Code / Indicator | Definition | Measurement Unit | Subgroups | | | | | | Departments | | | | | | Source Data | UNDP HDR | | Priority |
|---|---|---|---|---|---|---|---|---|---|---|---|---|---|---|---|---|---|---|
| | | | S | A | N | SN | H | G | F | W | C | Y | E | SN | | Indicator | Value (Y/N) | |
| Educational services | | | | | | | | | | | | | | | | | | |
| ED-039 Public schools | Number of public schools, in total and by level and number of students | Count | | | | | | | X | | X | X | | X | SEC | | | 1 |
| ED-040 Private schools | Number of private schools, in total and by level and number of students | Count | | | | | | | X | | X | X | | X | SEC | | | 1 |
| ED-041 Adult literacy centers and night schools | Number of adult literacy centers and night schools | Count | | | | | | | X | | X | X | | | *SEC* | | | 2 |
| ED-042 Special education schools | Number of special education schools | Count | | | | | | | X | | X | X | | X | *SEC* | | | 2 |
| ED-043 Vocational training centers | Number of vocational training centers | Count | | | | | | | X | | X | X | | X | SEC | | | 2 |
| ED-044 Universities | Number of universities | Count | | | | | | | X | | X | X | | X | SEC | | | 1 |
| ED-045 Teaching staff in schools | Number of teaching staff in schools, by education level and public/private sector | Count | X | | | | | | X | X | X | X | | X | SEC | | | 1 |
| ED-046 Administrative staff in schools | Number of administrative staff in schools, by education level and public/private sector | Count | X | | | | | | X | X | X | X | | X | SEC | | | 1 |
| ED-047 University faculty | Number of faculty members in universities | Count | X | | | | | | X | X | X | X | | X | SEC | | | 1 |
| ED-048 Teacher:pupil ratio | Average of ratio of teachers to pupils by level of education and type of school | Ratio | | | | | | | X | X | X | X | | X | *SEC* | | | 2 |

**Table 3.2—Summary List of Indicators by Domain**

| Code / Indicator | Definition | Measurement Unit | Subgroups S | A | N | SN | Departments H | G | F | W | C | Y | E | SN | Source Data | UNDP HDR Indicator | Value (Y/N) | Priority |
|---|---|---|---|---|---|---|---|---|---|---|---|---|---|---|---|---|---|---|
| **Health and Nutrition** | | | | | | | | | | | | | | | | | | |
| *Health infrastructure conditions* | | | | | | | | | | | | | | | | | | |
| HN-001 Population with sustainable access to improved water sources | Percentage of the population with reasonable access (availability of at least 20 liters a person per day from a source within 1 kilometer of the user's dwelling) to any of the following types of water supply for drinking: household connections, public standpipes, boreholes, protected dug wells, protected springs, and rainwater collection | Percentage | | | | | X | X | X | | | | | | FHS | X | N | 2 |
| HN-002 Population with access to improved sanitation utilities | Percentage of the population with access to adequate excreta-disposal facilities, such as a connection to a sewer or septic tank system, a pour-flush latrine, a simple pit latrine, or a ventilated improved pit latrine | Percentage | | | | | X | X | X | | | | | | FHS | X | N | 2 |
| HN-003 Population with sustainable access to affordable essential drugs | Percentage of the population for whom a minimum of 20 of the most essential drugs (those that satisfy the health care needs of the majority of the population) are continuously and affordably available at public or private health facilities or drug outlets within one hour's travel from home | Percentage | | | | | X | X | X | | | | | | NHA, HMC | X | Y | 2 |
| *Health services infrastructure* | | | | | | | | | | | | | | | | | | |
| HN-004 Public hospitals | Number of public hospitals divided by total population | Count, per 10,000 persons | | | | | | X | X | | | | X | | PC, NHA | | | 1 |
| HN-005 Public hospital beds | Number of beds in government hospitals divided by total population | Count, per 10,000 persons | | | | | | X | X | | | | X | | PC, NHA | | | 1 |
| HN-006 Private hospitals | Number of private hospitals divided by total population | Count, per 10,000 persons | | | | | | X | X | | | | X | | PC, NHA | | | 1 |
| HN-007 Public health centers | Number of public health centers divided by total population | Count, per 10,000 persons | | | | | | X | X | | | | X | | PC, NHA | | | 1 |
| HN-008 Outpatient clinics that are subsidiary to Hamad Medical Corporation | Number of outpatient clinics that are subsidiary to Hamad Medical Corporation divided by total population | Count, per 10,000 persons | | | | | | X | X | | | | X | | PC, NHA | | | 1 |
| HN-009 Armed Forces clinics | Number of Armed Forces clinics divided by total population | Count, per 10,000 persons | | | | | | X | X | | | | X | | PC, NHA | | | 1 |
| HN-010 Police clinics | Number of police clinics divided by total population | Count, per 10,000 persons | | | | | | X | X | | | | X | | PC, NHA | | | 1 |

Table 3.2—Summary List of Indicators by Domain

| Code / Indicator | Definition | Measurement Unit | Subgroups | | | | | | Departments | | | | | | Source Data | UNDP HDR | | Priority |
|---|---|---|---|---|---|---|---|---|---|---|---|---|---|---|---|---|---|---|
| | | | S | A | N | SN | H | G | F | W | C | Y | E | SN | | Indicator | Value (Y/N) | |
| HN-011 Qatar Petroleum clinics | Number of Qatar Petroleum clinics, divided by total population | Count, per 10,000 persons | | | | | | X | X | | | | X | | PC, NHA | | | 1 |
| HN-012 Private clinics and medical complexes | Number of clinics and medical complexes in the private sector, divided by total population | Count, per 10,000 persons | | | | | | X | X | | | | X | | PC, NHA | | | 1 |
| HN-013 Governmental primary health care units | Number of governmental primary health care units divided by total population | Count, per 10,000 persons | | | | | | X | X | | | | X | | PC, NHA | | | 1 |
| HN-014 Medical centers for athletes | Number of medical centers for athletes, divided by total population | Count, per 10,000 persons | | | | | | X | X | | | X | | | PC, NHA | | | 1 |
| HN-015 Specialized centers for the treatment and rehabilitation of drug addicts | Number of specialized centers for the treatment and rehabilitation of drug addicts divided by total population | Count, per 10,000 persons | | | | | | X | X | | | X | | | PC, NHA | | | 1 |
| HN-016 Psychotherapy centers | Number of psychotherapy centers divided by total population | Count, per 10,000 persons | | | | | | X | X | | | X | X | | PC, NHA | | | 1 |
| HN-017 Psychological counseling centers | Number of psychological counseling centers divided by total population | Count, per 10,000 persons | | | | | | X | X | | | X | X | | PC, NHA | | | 1 |
| HN-018 Physicians | Number of graduates of a faculty or school of medicine who are working in any medical field (including teaching, research, and practice), divided by total population | Count, per 10,000 persons | | | | | | X | X | | | X | X | | PC, NHA | X | Y | 1 |
| HN-019 Dentists | Number of dentists divided by total population | Count, per 10,000 persons | X | | | | | X | X | | | | X | | PC, NHA | | | 1 |
| HN-020 Nurses | Number of nurses (males and females) divided by total population | Count, per 10,000 persons | X | | | | | X | X | | | | X | | PC, NHA | | | 1 |
| HN-021 Pharmacists | Number of pharmacists divided by total population | Count, per 10,000 persons | X | | | | | X | X | | | | X | | PC, NHA | | | 1 |
| HN-022 Other health care providers | Number of people in other health care professions (other than doctors, dentists, nurses, and pharmacists), divided by total population | Count, per 10,000 persons | X | | | | | X | X | | | | X | | PC, NHA | | | 1 |

47

**Table 3.2—Summary List of Indicators by Domain**

| Code / Indicator | Definition | Measurement Unit | Subgroups S | A | N | SN | H | G | Departments F | W | C | Y | E | SN | Source Data | UNDP HDR Indicator | Value (Y/N) | Priority |
|---|---|---|---|---|---|---|---|---|---|---|---|---|---|---|---|---|---|---|
| *Health services utilization* | | | | | | | | | | | | | | | | | | |
| HN-023 Population who receive health services | Number of persons who receive health services in a given time period | Count | X | X | | | | | X | X | X | X | X | X | NHA | | | 2 |
| HN-024 Enrollees in psychological rehabilitation programs | Number of persons who enroll in psychological rehabilitation programs in a given time period | Count | X | X | | | | | X | X | X | X | X | X | NHA | | | 2 |
| HN-025 Population that receive treatment at governmental hospitals | Number of persons who receive treatment at government hospitals in a given time period | Count | X | X | | | | | X | X | X | X | X | X | NHA | | | 2 |
| HN-026 Population that receive treatment in private hospitals | Number of persons who receive treatment at private hospitals in a given time period | Count | X | X | | | | | X | X | X | X | X | X | NHA | | | 2 |
| HN-027 Population that receive medical treatment abroad | Number of persons who receive medical treatment abroad | Count | X | X | | | | | X | X | X | X | X | X | NHA | | | 2 |
| HN-028 Population that receive treatment in Qatar | Number of persons who receive medical treatment in Qatar | Count | X | X | | | | | X | X | X | X | X | X | NHA | | | 2 |
| HN-029 *Utilization rate of health services for acute conditions* | Number of persons seeking medical care (doctor, pharmacist, traditional healer) about their acute condition, divided by number reporting an acute condition in the last 2 weeks | Percentage | X | X | | | | | X | X | X | X | X | X | FHS | | | 1 |
| HN-030 Incidence of antenatal care | Percentage of pregnant women receiving medical care prior to birth (antenatal care) | Percentage | | X | | | | | X | X | X | | | | FHS, NHA | | | 1 |
| HN-031 Incidence of attended births | Number of deliveries attended by trained personnel (doctors, nurses, midwives) divided by the total number of births | Percentage | | X | | | | | X | X | X | | | | FHS, NHA | X | Y | 1 |
| HN-032 Incidence of post-partum care | Percentage of women receiving medical care during the 6 weeks after delivery (post-partum care) | Percentage | | X | | | | | X | X | | | | | FHS | | | 1 |
| HN-033 *Incidence of dental care* | Proportion of population who visited a dentist in the last 12 months | Percentage | X | X | | | | | X | X | X | X | X | X | FHS | | | 1 |
| *Preventative health services utilization* | | | | | | | | | | | | | | | | | | |
| HN-034 Children immunized in first year of age | Percentage of children under 1 year of age with basic vaccinations, in total and for specific diseases | Percentage | X | | X | | | | X | X | X | | | | PC, NHA | | | 1 |
| HN-035 *Children fully immunized* | Percentage of children 12–23 months who have received the full course of childhood immunizations | Percentage | X | | X | | | | X | X | X | | | | FHS | | | 1 |
| HN-036 Children fully vaccinated against polio | Percentage of children 12–23 months who have received the full course (3 doses) of polio vaccination | Percentage | X | | X | | | | X | X | X | | | | FHS | | | 1 |
| HN-037 *Children partially vaccinated against polio* | Percentage of children 12–23 months who have received the first dose of polio vaccination | Percentage | X | | X | | | | X | X | X | | | | FHS | | | 1 |
| HN-038 Children fully vaccinated against DPT | Percentage of children 12–23 months who have received the full course (3 doses) of DPT (diphtheria, Pertussis [whooping cough] and tetanus) vaccination | Percentage | X | | X | | | | X | X | X | | | | FHS | | | 1 |

Table 3.2—Summary List of Indicators by Domain

| Code / Indicator | Definition | Measurement Unit | Subgroups | | | | | | Departments | | | | | | Source Data | UNDP HDR | | Priority |
|---|---|---|---|---|---|---|---|---|---|---|---|---|---|---|---|---|---|---|
| | | | S | A | N | SN | H | G | F | W | C | Y | E | SN | | Indicator | Value (Y/N) | |
| HN-039 Children partially vaccinated against DPT | Percentage of children 12–23 months who have received the first dose of DPT (diphtheria, Pertussis [whooping cough] and tetanus) vaccination | Percentage | X | | X | | | | X | X | X | | | | FHS | X | | 1 |
| HN-040 Children vaccinated against measles | Percentage of children 12–23 months who have received the measles vaccination | Percentage | X | | X | | | | X | X | X | | | | FHS | X | Y | 1 |
| HN-041 Children vaccinated against tuberculosis | Percentage of children 12–23 months who have received the tuberculosis (BCGR) vaccination | Percentage | X | | X | | | | X | X | X | | | | FHS | X | Y | 1 |
| HN-042 Children fully vaccinated against hepatitis | Percentage of children 12–23 months who have received the full course (3 doses) of hepatitis vaccination | Percentage | X | | X | | | | X | X | X | | | | FHS | | | 1 |
| HN-043 Children partially vaccinated against hepatitis | Percentage of children 12–23 months who have received the first dose of hepatitis vaccination | Percentage | X | | X | | | | X | X | X | | | | FHS | | | 1 |
| **Health expenditures** | | | | | | | | | | | | | | | | | | |
| HN-044 Expenditure on public health as a percentage of GDP | Current and capital spending from government budgets, external borrowings, and grants (including donations from international agencies and nongovernmental organizations) and social (or compulsory) health insurance funds, divided by GDP | US$ million, percentage | | | | | | | X | | | | | | NHA | X | Y | 1 |
| HN-045 Expenditure on private health as a percentage of GDP | Direct household (out-of-pocket) spending, private insurance, spending by non-profit institutions serving households, and direct service payments by private corporations, divided by GDP | US$ million, percentage | | | | | | | X | | | | | | NHA, private-sector data | X | Y | 1 |
| HN-046 Per capita health expenditure | Sum of public and private health expenditures measured in PPP US$ divided by total population | PPP US$ | | | | | | | X | | | | | | NHA, private-sector data | X | Y | 1 |
| HN-047 Per capita health expenditure, total and by type | Sum of public and private health expenditures measured in QR, in total and separately by preventative care and treatment care, all divided by total population | QR decomposition | | | | | | | X | | | | | | NHA, private-sector data | | | 1 |
| HN-048 Per capita health expenditure on medicines, total and by type | Sum of public and private health expenditures on medicines measured in QR, in total and separately by preventative medicines versus curative medicines, all divided by total population | QR decomposition | | | | | | | X | | | | | | NHA, private-sector data | | | 2 |
| HN-049 Per capita health expenditure for special needs population, total and by type | Sum of public and private health expenditures for services for special needs population, measured in QR, in total and separately by treatment services versus rehabilitation services, all divided by number of special needs population | QR decomposition | | | | | | | X | | | | | X | NHA, private-sector data | | | 2 |

**Table 3.2—Summary List of Indicators by Domain**

| Code / Indicator | Definition | Measurement Unit | Subgroups S | A | N | SN | H | G | Departments F | W | C | Y | E | SN | Source Data | UNDP HDR Indicator | Value (Y/N) | Priority |
|---|---|---|---|---|---|---|---|---|---|---|---|---|---|---|---|---|---|---|
| **Nutritional status** | | | | | | | | | | | | | | | | | | |
| HN-050 Undermourished population | Percentage of the population whose food intake is chronically insufficient to meet their minimum energy requirements | Percentage | X | X | | | | | X | X | X | X | X | X | Household nutrition surveys | X | N | 4 |
| HN-051 Incidence of obesity | Percentage of the population whose body mass index exceeds the level that defines obesity | Percentage | X | X | | | | | X | X | X | X | X | X | Household nutrition surveys | | | 3 |
| HN-052 Infants with low birthweight | Number of births less than 2,500 grams divided by the total number of births | Percentage | X | X | | | | | X | X | X | | | | NHA | X | Y | 1 |
| HN-053 New mothers' vitamin A consumption | Percentage of new mothers who consume elements containing vitamin A before her newborn is 8 weeks | Percentage | | X | | | | | X | X | X | | | | Household nutrition surveys | | | 3 |
| HN-054 Children under age 5 under the appropriate weight for their age (wasting) | Percentage of children under age 5 who are 2 standard deviations or more below the median weight for age of the reference population | Percentage | X | X | | | | | X | X | X | | | | Household nutrition surveys | X | Y | 3 |
| HN-055 Children under age 5 under the appropriate height for their age (stunting) | Percentage of children under age 5 who are 2 standard deviations or more below the median height for age of the reference population | Percentage | X | X | | | | | X | X | X | | | | Household nutrition surveys | X | Y | 3 |
| HN-056 Prevalence of breastfeeding | Percent of all children born who were ever breastfed | Percentage | X | | | | | | X | X | X | | | | FHS | | | 1 |
| HN-057 Prevalence of exclusive breastfeeding | Percent of infants under four months of age who are exclusively or predominantly breastfed | Percentage | X | | | | | | X | X | X | | | | FHS | | | 1 |
| HN-058 Prevalence of breastfeeding continuation | Percent of children aged 12–15 months or 20–23 months who are still being breastfed | Percentage | X | | | | | | X | X | X | | | | FHS | | | 1 |
| HN-059 Mean duration of breastfeeding | Mean duration (in number of months) of breastfeeding | Months | X | | | | | | X | X | X | | | | FHS | | | 1 |
| HN-060 Children's vitamin A consumption | Percentage of children who eat food containing vitamin A | Percentage | X | X | | | | | X | X | X | | | | Household nutrition surveys | | | 3 |
| **Women's reproductive health** | | | | | | | | | | | | | | | | | | |
| HN-061 Contraceptive prevalence rate | The percentage of married women ages 15-49 who are using, or whose partners are using, any form of contraception, whether modern or traditional | Percentage | | X | | | | | X | X | | X | | | FHS | X | Y | 1 |
| HN-062 Contraceptive prevalence rates by method | The percentage of married women ages 15-49 who are using, or whose partners are using, specific forms of contraception or contraceptive methods (e.g., pill, IUD, injections, etc.) | Percentage | | X | | | | | X | X | | X | | | FHS | | | 1 |
| HN-063 Percentage using condom in the latest high-risk sexual intercourse | The fraction of men and women who respond that they used a condom the last time they had sex with a non-marital, non-cohabitating partner, of those who have had sex with such a partner in the last 12 months | Percentage | | X | | | | | X | X | | X | | | Household health surveys | X | N | 3 |

Table 3.2—Summary List of Indicators by Domain

| Code / Indicator | Definition | Measurement Unit | S | A | N | SN | H | G | F | W | C | Y | E | SN | Source Data | Indicator | Value (Y/N) | Priority |
|---|---|---|---|---|---|---|---|---|---|---|---|---|---|---|---|---|---|---|
| HN-064 Mothers vaccinated against natal polio | Percentage of mothers vaccinated against natal polio | Percentage | | X | | | | | X | X | | X | | | *NHA* | | | 3 |
| HN-065 Abortion rate | Number of abortions divided by live births | Per 1,000 live births | | X | | | | | X | X | | X | | | NHA | | | 1 |
| *Health behaviors* | | | | | | | | | | | | | | | | | | |
| HN-066 Iodine-treated salt consumption per capita | Total annual consumption of salt treated with iodine divided by total population | *Value per capita* | | | | | | | X | X | X | X | X | X | *Administrative data, national accounts* | | | 3 |
| HN-067 Cigarette consumption per capita | Total annual consumption of cigarettes divided by total population | Value per capita | X | X | | | | | X | X | X | X | X | X | *Administrative data, national accounts* | | | 2 |
| HN-068 *Smoking prevalence* | Percentage of population who smoke cigarettes | Percentage | X | X | | | | | X | X | X | | | | FHS | X | N | 1 |
| HN-069 *Drug use prevalence* | Percentage of population who use drugs from a specified list of legal or illegal substances | Percentage | X | X | | | | | X | X | X | X | | | *Household / health surveys* | | | 3 |
| HN-070 *Drug treatment rate* | Ratio of individuals treated for drug use divided by the total number of drug users | Percentage | X | X | | | | | X | X | X | X | | | *Household / health surveys, HMC* | | | 3 |
| *Domestic violence* | | | | | | | | | | | | | | | | | | |
| HN-071 *Abuse cases reported by type* | Cases of domestic violence in total and by type | Count, Percentage | X | | | | | | X | X | X | | | | MIA | | | 2 |
| *Diseases* | | | | | | | | | | | | | | | | | | |
| HN-072 Incidence of measles cases | Total number of measles cases divided by population | Per 100,000 persons | X | X | | | | | X | X | X | X | X | | PC, NHA | | | 1 |
| HN-073 Incidence of polio cases | Total number of polio cases divided by population | Per 100,000 persons | X | X | | | | | X | X | X | X | X | | PC, NHA | | | 1 |
| HN-074 Incidence of malaria cases | Total number of malaria cases reported to the World Health Organization by countries in which malaria is endemic, divided by population | Per 100,000 persons | X | X | | | | | X | X | X | X | X | | PC, NHA | X | N | 2 |
| HN-075 Incidence of tuberculosis cases | Total number of tuberculosis cases reported to the World Health Organization, divided by population | Per 100,000 persons | X | X | | | | | X | X | X | X | X | | PC, NHA | X | Y | 1 |
| HN-076 Tuberculosis cases detected under DOTS (directly observed treatment, short course) | Percentage of estimated new infectious tuberculosis cases detected (diagnosed in a given period) under the DOTS case detection and treatment strategy | Percentage | X | X | | | | | X | X | X | X | X | | NHA | X | Y | 2 |
| HN-077 Tuberculosis cases cured under DOTS | Percentage of estimated new infectious tuberculosis cases cured under the DOTS case detection and treatment strategy | Percentage | X | X | | | | | X | X | X | X | X | | NHA | X | Y | 2 |
| HN-078 Incidence of low level of urinary iodine | Percentage of the population infected with low level of urinary iodine | Percentage | X | X | | | | | X | X | X | X | X | | NHA | X | | 3 |

Table 3.2—Summary List of Indicators by Domain

| Code / Indicator | Definition | Measurement Unit | Subgroups | | | | | | Departments | | | | | | Source Data | UNDP HDR | | Priority |
|---|---|---|---|---|---|---|---|---|---|---|---|---|---|---|---|---|---|---|
| | | | S | A | N | SN | H | G | F | W | C | Y | E | SN | | Indicator | Value (Y/N) | |
| HN-079 Incidence of diarrhea in children | Percentage of children under age 5 with diarrhea in the last 24 hours (or last 2 weeks) | Percentage | X | X | | | | | X | X | X | | | | FHS, NHA | | | 2 |
| HN-080 Incidence of tetanus in newborns | Percentage of children infected with tetanus that usually affects newborn | Percentage | X | X | | | | | X | X | X | | | | NHA | | | 2 |
| HN-081 Incidence of night blindness in children | Percentage of children infected with night blindness (due to vitamin A deficiency) | Percentage | X | X | | | | | X | X | X | | | | NHA | | | 2 |
| HN-082 Incidence of inflation of the thyroid in children | Inflation of the thyroid among children | Percentage | X | X | | | | | X | X | X | | | | NHA | | | 2 |
| HN-083 Children under age 5 ill with fever in 2 weeks prior to survey and treated with anti-malaria drugs | Percentage of children under age 5 ill with fever in 2 weeks prior to survey and treated with anti-malarial drugs | Percentage | X | X | | | | | X | X | X | | | | NHA | X | N | 4 |
| HN-084 Children under age 5 sleeping under insecticide-treated bed nets | Percentage of children under age 5 sleeping under insecticide-treated bed nets | Percentage | X | X | | | | | X | X | X | | | | NHA | X | N | 4 |
| HN-085 Incidence of vitamin A deficiency in children | Percentage of children who have deficiency in vitamin A | Percentage | X | X | | | | | X | X | X | | | | NHA | | | 2 |
| HN-086 Incidence of HIV/AIDS | Percentage of people ages 15–49 who are infected with HIV/AIDS | Count, rate | X | X | | | | | X | X | X | X | X | | NHA | X | N | 1 |
| HN-087 Incidence of HIV/AIDS in pregnant women | Percentage of pregnant women infected with HIV/AIDS | Percentage | | X | | | | | X | X | | | | | NHA | | | 1 |
| HN-088 Incidence of night blindness in pregnant women | Percentage of pregnant women afflicted with night blindness (due to vitamin A deficiency) | Percentage | | X | | | | | X | X | | | | | NHA | | | 2 |
| HN-089 Incidence of anemia in pregnant women | Percentage of pregnant women afflicted with anemia | Percentage | | X | | | | | X | X | | | | | NHA | | | 2 |
| HN-090 Incidence of diarrhea | Percentage of people with diarrhea in the last two weeks | Percentage | X | X | | | | | X | X | X | X | X | | NHA, FHS | | | 1 |
| HN-091 Incidence of high blood pressure | Percentage of people who report they have ever had high blood pressure | Percentage | X | X | | | | | X | X | X | X | X | | FHS | | | 1 |
| HN-092 Incidence of heart disease | Percentage of people who report they have ever had heart disease | Percentage | X | X | | | | | X | X | X | X | X | | FHS | | | 1 |
| HN-093 Incidence of cancer | Percentage of people who report they have ever had cancer | Percentage | X | X | | | | | X | X | X | X | X | | FHS | | | 1 |
| HN-094 Incidence of diabetes | Percentage of people who report they have ever had diabetes | Percentage | X | X | | | | | X | X | X | X | X | | FHS | | | 1 |
| HN-095 Rate of diabetics using insulin | Percentage of people who report they have ever had diabetes who currently inject insulin | Percentage | X | X | | | | | X | X | X | X | X | | FHS | | | 1 |
| HN-096 Incidence of asthma | Percentage of people who report they have ever had asthma | Percentage | X | X | | | | | X | X | X | X | X | | FHS | | | 1 |
| HN-097 Incidence of chronic geriatric diseases | Percentage of the population afflicted with specified chronic geriatric diseases | Percentage | X | X | | | | | | | | | X | | NHA | | | 2 |

**Table 3.2—Summary List of Indicators by Domain**

| Code / Indicator | Definition | Measurement Unit | Subgroups S | A | N | SN | H | G | Departments F | W | C | Y | E | SN | Source Data | UNDP HDR Indicator | Value (Y/N) | Priority |
|---|---|---|---|---|---|---|---|---|---|---|---|---|---|---|---|---|---|---|
| HN-098 Incidence of physical disabilities | Percentage of people who report they have a physical limitation that limits participation in normal activities for a person their age | Percentage | X | X | X | | | | | | | | X | X | FHS, Census | | | 1 |
| HN-099 Incidence of mental disabilities | Percentage of people who report they have a mental limitation that limits participation in normal activities for a person their age | Percentage | X | X | X | | | | | | | | X | X | FHS, Census | | | 1 |
| Special needs services | | | | | | | | | | | | | | | | | | |
| HN-100 Employment at special needs centers | Number of persons employed in centers serving people with special needs | Count | X | X | | X | | | | | | | | X | PC | | | 1 |
| HN-101 Employment at Al-Noor Institute | Number of persons employed at Al-Noor Institute | Count | X | X | | X | | | | | | | | X | PC | | | 1 |
| HN-102 Faculty in special education schools | Number of faculty members working in special education schools | Count | X | X | | X | | | | | | | | X | SEC | | | 1 |
| HN-103 Health care utilization for special needs population | Number of persons with special needs who receive health services | Count | X | X | | X | | | | | | | | X | NHA, registries | | | 1 |
| HN-104 Residents in hospitals, special needs | Number of persons with special needs who are residents in hospitals | Count | X | X | | X | | | | | | | | X | NHA, registries | | | 1 |
| HN-105 Physical therapy, special needs | Number of persons with special needs who are receiving physical therapy | Count | X | X | | X | | | | | | | | X | NHA, registries | | | 1 |
| HN-106 Occupational therapy, special needs | Number of persons with special needs who are receiving occupational therapy | Count | X | X | | X | | | | | | | | X | NHA, registries | | | 1 |
| HN-107 Rehabilitation treatment, special needs | Number of persons with special needs who are receiving rehabilitation treatment | Count | X | X | | X | | | | | | | | X | NHA, registries | | | 1 |

Table 3.2—Summary List of Indicators by Domain

| Code / Indicator | Definition | Measurement Unit | Subgroups S | A | N | SN | H | G | Departments F | W | C | Y | E | SN | Source Data | UNDP HDR Indicator | Value (Y/N) | Priority |
|---|---|---|---|---|---|---|---|---|---|---|---|---|---|---|---|---|---|---|
| **Environment** | | | | | | | | | | | | | | | | | | |
| *Geography of the state* | | | | | | | | | | | | | | | | | | |
| EV-001 Land area covered by forests | Total land area covered by forests divided by total land area | Percentage | | | | | | | X | | | | | | PC | | | 3 |
| EV-002 *Rate of land desertification* | Annual rate of change in land area covered by forests | Value | | | | | | | X | | | | | | PC | | | 3 |
| EV-003 Protected land area | Total protected land area divided by total land area | Percentage | | | | | | | X | | | | | | PC | | | 3 |
| *Air* | | | | | | | | | | | | | | | | | | |
| EV-004 Carbon dioxide emissions per capita | Human-originated carbon dioxide emissions stemming from burning of fossil fuels, gas flaring, and production of cement divided by the population | Metric tons | | | | | | | X | | | | | | *Administrative records* | X | Y | 3 |
| EV-005 Share of world carbon dioxide emissions | Human-originated carbon dioxide emissions stemming from burning of fossil fuels, gas flaring, and production of cement divided by world total emissions | Percentage | | | | | | | X | | | | | | *Administrative records* | X | Y | 3 |
| EV-006 Consumption of ozone-depleting chlorofluorocarbons | Human-originated consumption of ozone-depleting chlorofluorocarbons (ozone depletion potential [ODP] metric tons) | Metric tons | | | | | | | X | | | | | | *Administrative records* | | | 3 |
| *Water* | | | | | | | | | | | | | | | | | | |
| EV-007 *Water production by type (extraction, desalination)* | Quantity of water produced using various methods (e.g., well field, desalination plants) | Value | | | | | | | X | | | | | | PC | | | 2 |
| EV-008 *Seashore pollution* | To be determined | Value | | | | | | | X | | | | | | *Administrative records* | | | 3 |
| *Energy* | | | | | | | | | | | | | | | | | | |
| EV-009 Electricity consumption per capita | Gross production of electricity (kilowatt hours) divided by the total population | Kilowatt hours per person | | | | | | | X | | | | | | PC | X | Y | 2 |
| EV-010 Share of energy consumption in traditional fuels | Consumption of traditional fuels (fuel wood, charcoal, sugar cane waster, animal, vegetal, and other wastes) divided by total energy consumed | Percentage | | | | | | | X | | | | | | *Administrative records* | X | Y | 2 |
| EV-011 GDP per unit of energy use | GDP in PPP US$ divided by commercial energy use measured in kilograms of oil equivalent | Ratio | | | | | | | X | | | | | | PC | X | N | 3 |

Table 3.2—Summary List of Indicators by Domain

| Code / Indicator | Definition | Measurement Unit | Subgroups | | | | | | | | Departments | | | | Source Data | UNDP HDR | | Priority |
|---|---|---|---|---|---|---|---|---|---|---|---|---|---|---|---|---|---|---|
| | | | S | A | N | SN | H | G | F | W | C | Y | E | SN | | Indicator | Value (Y/N) | |
| **Civil and Political Life** | | | | | | | | | | | | | | | | | | |
| **Cultural activities** | | | | | | | | | | | | | | | | | | |
| C-001 Public libraries | Number of public libraries | Count | | | | | | X | X | | X | X | X | | PC | | | 1 |
| C-002 Newspapers | Number of newspapers | Count | | | | | | X | X | | | X | | | PC | | | 1 |
| C-003 Monthly magazines | Number of monthly magazines | Count | | | | | | X | X | | | X | | | PC | | | 1 |
| C-004 Movie theaters | Number of movie theaters | Count | | | | | | X | X | | | X | | | PC | | | 1 |
| C-005 Clubs, associations and cooperatives | Total number of clubs, associations and cooperatives | Count | | | | | | X | X | | X | X | X | | PC | | | 1 |
| C-006 Social and cultural clubs | Number of social and cultural clubs | Count | | | | | | X | X | | | X | X | | PC | | | 1 |
| C-007 Scientific clubs | Number of scientific clubs | Count | | | | | | X | X | | | X | | | PC | | | 1 |
| C-008 *Women's associations and unions* | Number of women's associations and unions | Count | | | | | | | X | X | | | | | *Registries, administrative records* | | | 1 |
| C-009 Disabled people participating in cultural activities | The number disabled people participating in cultural activities | Count | | | | X | | | | | | | | X | *Registries, administrative records* | | | 1 |
| C-010 Youth participating in non-sport activities | Number of share of youth participating in non-sport activities (e.g., religious, cultural, scientific, creative, or performing arts) | Count, percentage | X | X | | | | | | | X | X | | | PC | | | 1 |
| C-011 Youth establishments | Total number of youth establishments | Count | | | | | | | | | X | X | | | PC | | | 1 |
| C-012 Youth centers | Number of youth centers | Count | | | | | | | | | X | X | | | PC | | | 1 |
| C-013 Youth centers associations | Number of youth centers associations | Count | | | | | | | | | X | X | | | PC | | | 1 |
| **Athletic activities** | | | | | | | | | | | | | | | | | | |
| C-014 Players registered in sports clubs | Number of players registered in sports clubs | Count | X | X | | | | | | | X | X | | | PC | | | 1 |
| C-015 Sports clubs | Number of sport and cultural clubs and sports clubs (second class) | Count | | | | | | | | | X | X | | | PC | | | 1 |
| C-016 Sports unions | Number of sports unions | Count | | | | | | | | | X | X | | | PC | | | 1 |
| C-017 Sports clubs and societies | Number of specialized sport clubs and societies | Count | | | | | | | | | X | X | | | PC | | | 1 |

55

**Table 3.2—Summary List of Indicators by Domain**

| Code / Indicator | Definition | Measurement Unit | Subgroups | | | | | | Departments | | | | | | Source Data | UNDP HDR | | Priority |
|---|---|---|---|---|---|---|---|---|---|---|---|---|---|---|---|---|---|---|
| | | | S | A | N | SN | H | G | F | W | C | Y | E | SN | | Indicator | Value (Y/N) | |
| **Women's political participation** | | | | | | | | | | | | | | | | | | |
| C-018 Women's share of eligible voters in municipal council elections | Number of eligible voters in municipal council election who are women, divided by total number of eligible voters | Percentage | | | | | | | | X | | X | | | MIA | | | 1 |
| C-019 Women's share of voters in municipal council elections | For a given municipal council election, number of women voters who participated in the election, divided by the total number of voters who participated in the election | Percentage | | | | | | | | X | | X | | | MIA | | | 1 |
| C-020 Women candidates for municipal council | For a given municipal council election, number of women candidates for council membership | Count | | | | | | | | X | | X | | | MIA | | | 1 |
| C-021 Women elected to municipal council | For a given municipal council election, number of women elected to council membership | Count | | | | | | | | X | | X | | | MIA | | | 1 |
| C-022 Year women received right to vote | The calendar year women first received the right to vote on a universal and equal basis | Year | | | | | | | | X | | X | | | *MIA* | X | Y | 1 |
| C-023 Year women received right to stand for election | The calendar year women were given the right to run for office as a candidate on a universal and equal basis | Year | | | | | | | | X | | X | | | *MIA* | X | Y | 1 |
| C-024 Year the first woman was elected or appointed as a member of parliament | The calendar year a woman was elected or appointed as a member of parliament | Year | | | | | | | | X | | X | | | *MIA* | X | Y | 1 |
| C-025 Women's share of parliamentary seats in lower or single house | Number of parliamentary seats in lower or single house occupied by women, divided by the number of parliamentary seats | Percentage | | | | | | | | X | | X | | | *MIA* | X | Y | 1 |
| C-026 Women's share of parliamentary seats in upper house or senate | Number of parliamentary seats in upper house or senate occupied by women divided by the number of parliamentary seats | Percentage | | | | | | | | X | | X | | | *MIA* | X | Y | 1 |
| C-027 Women's share of government ministerial positions | Number of women in ministerial level positions in government divided by the total number of ministerial positions | Percentage | | | | | | | | X | | X | | | MCSAH | X | Y | 1 |
| C-028 Women's share of employment in NGOs | Number of women employees in nongovernmental organizations (NGOs) divided by the total number of NGO employees | Percentage | | | | | | | | X | | X | | | *Private-sector administrative data* | | | 1 |
| C-029 *Women's share of managers in public and private institutions* | Number of women managers in public and private institutions, divided by total number of managers in these institutions | Percentage | | | | | | | | X | | X | | | PC | | | 1 |

56

**Table 3.2—Summary List of Indicators by Domain**

| Code / Indicator | Definition | Measurement Unit | Subgroups | | | | | | Departments | | | | | | Source Data | UNDP HDR | | Priority |
|---|---|---|---|---|---|---|---|---|---|---|---|---|---|---|---|---|---|---|
| | | | S | A | N | SN | H | G | F | W | C | Y | E | SN | | Indicator | Value (Y/N) | |
| **Safety and Security** | | | | | | | | | | | | | | | | | | |
| **National security** | | | | | | | | | | | | | | | | | | |
| SS-001 Total of armed forces | Strategic, land, naval, air, command, administrative, and support forces; paramilitary forces included if trained in military tactics | Thousands, index (1985=100) | | | | | | | X | | | | | | *AF* | X | Y | 3 |
| SS-002 Conventional arms imports | Voluntary transfer (imports) of weapons with a military purpose, including ships, aircraft, missiles, artillery, armored vehicles, and guidance and radar systems | US$ millions (1990 prices) | | | | | | | X | | | | | | *National accounts, PC* | X | Y | 3 |
| SS-003 Conventional arms exports | Voluntary transfer (exports) of weapons with a military purpose, including ships, aircraft, missiles, artillery, armored vehicles and radar systems | US$ millions (1990 prices) | | | | | | | X | | | | | | *National accounts, PC* | X | N | 4 |
| **National security expenditures** | | | | | | | | | | | | | | | | | | |
| SS-004 Military expenditures | All expenditures of the defense ministry and other ministries on recruiting and training military personnel, as well as on construction and purchase of military supplies and equipment, divided by GDP | Percentage | | | | | | | X | | | | | | *National accounts, PC* | X | N | 4 |
| **Crime** | | | | | | | | | | | | | | | | | | |
| SS-005 *Homicide rate* | Number of reported homicides in a year divided by the total population | Number per 100,000 persons | X | X | | | | | X | X | X | X | X | X | *MIA* | | | 2 |
| SS-006 *Crime victimization rates* | Number of people who report that they have been victimized, in total and by certain types of crime (property, robbery, sexual assault, assault, bribery, and so on), in the preceding year, divided by the population | Number per 100,000 persons | X | X | | | | | X | X | X | X | X | X | *MIA* | | | 2 |
| SS-007 *Rate of juvenile delinquency* | Number of juveniles with contact with the criminal justice system (e.g., arrests, charges, convictions) divided by the total number of juveniles | Number per 100,000 persons | X | X | | | | | | | X | X | | | *MIA* | | | 1 |
| SS-008 *Drug share of illegal seizures* | Ratio of value of drugs seized to value of all seized illegal products | Ratio | | | | | | | X | | X | | | | *MIA* | | | 2 |
| SS-009 *Drug share of convictions* | Ratio of persons imprisoned or fined for using or selling drugs to all convictions | Ratio | | | | | | | X | | X | | | | *MIA* | | | 2 |

57

**Table 3.2—Summary List of Indicators by Domain**

| Code / Indicator | Definition | Measurement Unit | Subgroups S | A | N | SN | H | G | Depts F | W | C | Y | E | SN | Source Data | UNDP HDR Indicator | Value (Y/N) | Priority |
|---|---|---|---|---|---|---|---|---|---|---|---|---|---|---|---|---|---|---|
| **Accidents** | | | | | | | | | | | | | | | | | | |
| SS-010 *Automobile accidents* | Annual number of automobile accidents | Count | X | X | | | | | X | | | X | | | PC | | | 1 |
| SS-011 *Fatal automobile accidents* | Annual number of automobile accidents that involve a fatality | Count | X | X | | | | | X | | | X | | | PC | | | 1 |
| SS-012 *Automobile accident fatalities* | Annual number of fatalities from automobile accidents | Count | X | X | | | | | X | | | X | | | PC | | | 1 |
| SS-013 *Youth share of automobile accidents* | Ratio of automobile accidents involving a youth driver (age range to be determined) to total automobile accidents | Percentage | X | X | | | | | X | | | X | | | *PC* | | | 1 |
| SS-014 *Youth share of fatal automobile accidents* | Ratio of fatal automobile accidents involving a youth driver (age range to be determined) to total fatal automobile accidents | Percentage | X | X | | | | | X | | | X | | | *PC* | | | 1 |
| SS-015 *Youth share of automobile accident fatalities* | Ratio of youth (age range to be determined) fatalities from automobile accidents to total automobile accident fatalities | Percentage | X | X | | | | | X | | | X | | | PC | | | 1 |
| **Immigration** | | | | | | | | | | | | | | | | | | |
| SS-016 *Women's share among immigrants* | Number of women immigrants divided by total immigrants | Count, Percentage | X | X | | | | | X | X | | | | | *Migrant registries* | | | 2 |
| SS-017 *Women's share among emigrants* | Number of women emigrants divided by total emigrants | Count, Percentage | X | X | | | | | X | X | | | | | *Migrant registries* | | | 2 |
| **Refugees** | | | | | | | | | | | | | | | | | | |
| SS-018 *Internally displaced persons* | Number of people who are displaced within their own country and to whom the United Nations High Commissioner for Refugees extends protection or assistance, or both, generally pursuant to a special request by a competent organ of the United Nations | Thousands | X | X | | | | | X | X | | | | | *MIA* | X | Y | 4 |
| SS-019 *Refugees by country of asylum* | Number of people who have fled their country because of a well-founded fear of persecution and living in Qatar | Thousands | X | X | | | | | X | X | | | | | *Migrant registries* | X | N | 4 |
| SS-020 *Refugees by country of origin* | Number of people who have fled Qatar because of a well-founded fear of persecution | Thousands | X | X | | | | | X | X | | | | | *Migrant registries* | X | N | 4 |

**Table 3.2—Summary List of Indicators by Domain**

| Code / Indicator | Definition | Measurement Unit | Subgroups | | | | | | Departments | | | | | | Source Data | UNDP HDR | | Priority |
|---|---|---|---|---|---|---|---|---|---|---|---|---|---|---|---|---|---|---|
| | | | S | A | N | SN | H | G | F | W | C | Y | E | SN | | Indicator | Value (Y/N) | |
| | | | Statutory | | | | | | | | | | | | | | | |
| **Conventions** | | | | | | | | | | | | | | | | | | |
| ST-001 International Convention on the Elimination of All Forms of Racial Discrimination, 1965 | Stated convention | | | | | | | | X | | | | | | Document | X | Y | 1 |
| ST-002 International Covenant on Civil and Political Rights, 1966 | Stated convention | | | | | | | | X | | | | | | Document | X | Y | 1 |
| ST-003 International Covenant on Economic, Social and Cultural Rights, 1966 | Stated convention | | | | | | | | X | | | | | | Document | X | Y | 1 |
| ST-004 Convention of Elimination of All Forms of Discrimination Against Women, 1979 | Stated convention | | | | | | | | X | X | | | | | Document | X | Y | 1 |
| ST-005 Convention Against Torture and Other Cruel, Inhuman or Degrading Treatment or Punishment, 1984 | Stated convention | | | | | | | | X | | | | | | Document | X | Y | 1 |
| ST-006 Convention on Rights of the Child, 1989 | Stated convention | | | | | | | | | | X | | | | Document | X | Y | 1 |
| ST-007 International Convention on the Rights of Persons with Disabilities | Stated convention | | | | | | | | | | | | | X | Document | | | 1 |
| **Labor rights conventions** | | | | | | | | | | | | | | | | | | |
| ST-008 Freedom of association and collective bargaining—Convention 98 | Stated convention | | | | | | | | X | X | | | | | Document | X | Y | 1 |
| ST-009 Elimination of forced and compulsory labor—Convention 29 | Stated convention | | | | | | | | X | X | | | | | Document | X | Y | 1 |
| ST-010 Elimination of discrimination in respect of employment and occupation—Convention 111 | Stated convention | | | | | | | | X | X | | | | X | Document | X | Y | 1 |
| ST-011 Abolishing child labor—Conventions 138 and 182 | Stated convention | | | | | | | | | | X | | | | Document | X | Y | 1 |

**Table 3.2—Summary List of Indicators by Domain**

| Code / Indicator | Definition | Measurement Unit | Subgroups | | | | | | Departments | | | | | | Source Data | UNDP HDR | | Priority |
|---|---|---|---|---|---|---|---|---|---|---|---|---|---|---|---|---|---|---|
| | | | S | A | N | SN | H | G | F | W | C | Y | E | SN | | Indicator | Value (Y/N) | |
| Ratification of Environmental Treaties | | | | | | | | | | | | | | | | | | |
| ST-0012 Cartagena Protocol on Biosafety, 2000 | Stated treaty | | | | | | | | X | | | | | | Document | X | Y | 1 |
| ST-0013 Framework Convention on Climate Change, 1992 | Stated treaty | | | | | | | | X | | | | | | Document | X | Y | 1 |
| ST-0014 Kyoto Protocol to the Framework Convention on Climate Change, 1997 | Stated treaty | | | | | | | | X | | | | | | Document | X | Y | 1 |
| ST-0015 Convention on Biological Diversity, 1992 | Stated treaty | | | | | | | | X | | | | | | Document | X | Y | 1 |

NOTES: Indicators or units of measurement that were not listed in the QSCFA prototype database as of March 2004 are shown in italics. For subgroups: S=sex, A=age group, N=nationality, SN=special needs, H=headship or marital status, G=geography. For departments: F=Family, W=Women, C=Childhood, Y=Youth, E=Elderly, SN=Special Needs. For data sources: AF=Qatar Armed Forces, FHS=Qatar Family Health Survey, HEIS=Qatar Household Expenditure and Income Survey, HMC=Hamad Medical Corporation, LFS=Qatar Labour Force Survey, MCSAH=Qatar Ministry of Civil Service Affairs and Housing, MIA=Qatar Ministry of Interior Affairs, NHA=Qatar National Health Authority, PC=Qatar Planning Council, QF=Qatar Foundation, SEC=Qatar Supreme Education Council, UNDP=United Nations Development Programme, VS=Qatar vital statistics. UNDP HDR=United Nations Development Programme *Human Development Report* . Priority scale ranking is from 1 (highest) to 4 (lowest).

## Table 3.3—Summary List of Indicators by QSCFA Goals

| Code / Indicator | | Priority | Family well-being Goal 1–3 | Charters on family affairs Goal 4 | Women's empower-ment Goal 5 | Women's work Goal 6 | Support those with special needs Goal 7 | Youth challenges Goal 9 |
|---|---|---|---|---|---|---|---|---|
| | | | | | Population | | | |
| Population structure | | | | | | | | |
| P-001 | Total population | 1 | X | | X | | X | X |
| P-002 | *Total population distribution* | 1 | X | | X | | X | X |
| P-003 | Urban population | 1 | X | | X | | X | X |
| P-004 | *Dependency ratio* | 1 | X | | X | | X | X |
| P-005 | *Median age* | 1 | X | | X | | X | X |
| P-006 | *Population density* | 1 | X | | X | | X | X |
| P-007 | Registered disabled persons | 1 | X | | X | | X | |
| P-008 | Self-reported disabled persons | 1 | X | | X | | X | |
| Population growth | | | | | | | | |
| P-009 | Annual population growth rate | 1 | X | | X | | | |
| P-010 | Rate of natural increase | 1 | X | | X | | | |
| P-011 | Registered live births | 1 | X | | X | | | |
| P-012 | Crude birth rate | 1 | X | | X | | | X |
| P-013 | *General birth rate* | 1 | X | | X | | | X |
| P-014 | Total fertility rate | 1 | X | X | X | | | X |
| P-015 | *Median age at first birth* | 1 | X | | X | | | X |
| P-016 | Crude death rate | 1 | X | | X | | X | X |
| P-017 | *Cause-specific mortality* | 1 | X | | X | | X | X |
| P-018 | Infant mortality rate | 1 | X | X | X | | | |
| P-019 | Under age 5 child mortality rate | 1 | X | X | X | | | |
| P-020 | Maternal mortality rate | 1 | X | X | X | | | |
| Life expectancy | | | | | | | | |
| P-021 | Life expectancy at birth | 1 | X | X | X | | X | X |
| P-022 | Life expectancy index | 1 | X | X | X | | | X |
| P-023 | Survival rate to age 40 | 1 | X | X | X | | | X |
| P-025 | Survival rate to age 65 | 1 | X | X | X | | | X |

61

## Table 3.3—Summary List of Indicators by QSCFA Goals

| Code / Indicator | | Priority | Family well-being<br>Goal 1–3 | Charters on family affairs<br>Goal 4 | Women's empowerment<br>Goal 5 | Women's work<br>Goal 6 | Support those with special needs<br>Goal 7 | Youth challenges<br>Goal 9 |
|---|---|---|---|---|---|---|---|---|
| | | | Economy | | | | | |
| Overall economic activity | | | | | | | | |
| E-001 | GDP index | 1 | X | | | | | |
| E-002 | GDP | 1 | X | | | | | |
| E-003 | GDP per capita | 1 | X | | | | | |
| E-005 | GDP per capita annual growth rate | 1 | X | | | | | |
| E-006 | GDP per capita rank minus HDI rank | 1 | X | | | | | |
| E-007 | GDP per capita, highest value between years X and Y | 1 | X | | | | | |
| E-008 | GDP per capita, year of highest value | 1 | X | | | | | |
| E-009 | *Gross national income* | 1 | X | | | | | |
| E-010 | *Consumption GDP share* | 2 | X | | | | | |
| E-011 | *Investment GDP share* | 2 | X | | | | | |
| E-012 | *Savings GDP share* | 2 | X | | | | | |
| E-013 | Total debt services trade share | 2 | X | | | | | |
| E-014 | Total debt service GDP share | 2 | X | | | | | |
| E-015 | Net foreign direct investment inflows GDP share | 2 | X | | | | | |
| E-016 | Other private flows GDP share | 2 | X | | | | | |
| E-017 | *GDP implicit price deflator* | 1 | X | | | | | |
| E-018 | *Level of the Consumer Price Index (CPI)* | 1 | X | | | | | |
| E-019 | Annual inflation rate (CPI-linked) | 1 | X | | | | | |
| International trade | | | | | | | | |
| E-020 | Imports of goods and services GDP share | 2 | X | | | | | |
| E-021 | Exports of goods and services GDP share | 2 | X | | | | | |
| E-022 | Primary exports share | 2 | X | | | | | |
| E-023 | Manufactured exports share | 2 | X | | | | | |
| E-024 | High-technology exports share | 2 | X | | | | | |
| E-025 | Terms of trade | 2 | X | | | | | |

62

## Table 3.3—Summary List of Indicators by QSCFA Goals

| Code / Indicator | | Priority | Family well-being<br>Goal 1–3 | Charters on family affairs<br>Goal 4 | Women's empower-ment<br>Goal 5 | Women's work<br>Goal 6 | Support those with special needs<br>Goal 7 | Youth challenges<br>Goal 9 |
|---|---|---|---|---|---|---|---|---|
| **Human development indicators** | | | | | | | | |
| E-026 | Human development index (HDI) | 1 | X | | X | | | |
| E-027 | Gender-related development index (GDI) | 2 | X | X | X | | | X |
| E-028 | Gender-empowerment measure (GEM) | 2 | X | X | X | | | X |
| E-029 | HDI rank minus GDI rank | 2 | X | | X | | | |
| **Development assistance** | | | | | | | | |
| E-030 | Total net Official Development Assistance (ODA) received | 2 | X | | | | | |
| E-031 | Net ODA received per capita | 2 | X | | | | | |
| E-032 | Net ODA received GDP share | 2 | X | | | | | |
| **Technology** | | | | | | | | |
| E-033 | Telephone mainlines and cellular subscribers | 1 | X | | | | | X |
| E-034 | Telephone mainlines | 1 | X | | | | | X |
| E-035 | Cellular subscribers | 1 | X | | | | | X |
| E-037 | Internet users | 1 | X | | | | | X |
| E-038 | Personal computers in use | 1 | X | | | | | X |
| E-039 | *Radio access in households* | 2 | X | | | | | |
| E-040 | *TV access in households* | 2 | X | | | | | |
| E-041 | *Fixed-line telephone access in households* | 2 | X | | | | | |
| E-042 | *Cellular access in households* | 2 | X | | | | | |
| E-043 | *Computer use in households* | 2 | X | | | | | |
| E-044 | *Internet access in households* | 2 | X | | | | | |
| E-045 | *Business computer use* | 1 | X | | | | | |
| E-046 | *Business Internet use* | 1 | X | | | | | |
| E-047 | *Employee computer use* | 1 | X | | | | | |
| E-048 | *Employee Internet use* | 1 | X | | | | | |
| E-049 | Patents granted to residents | | | | | | | |
| E-050 | Receipts of royalties and license fees | 2 | X | | | | | |
| E-051 | Expenditure on research and development (R&D) GDP share | 2 | X | | | | | |

Table 3.3—Summary List of Indicators by QSCFA Goals

| Code / Indicator | | Priority | Family well-being Goal 1–3 | Charters on family affairs Goal 4 | Women's empower-ment Goal 5 | Women's work Goal 6 | Support those with special needs Goal 7 | Youth challenges Goal 9 |
|---|---|---|---|---|---|---|---|---|
| **Labor force** | | | | | | | | |
| E-052 | *Economically active population* | 1 | X | | X | X | X | X |
| E-053 | Rate of economic activity among the population | 1 | X | | X | X | X | X |
| E-054 | Annual growth rate of the labor force | 1 | X | | | | | |
| E-055 | *Retired population* | 1 | X | | X | X | | |
| E-056 | Retirement rate | 1 | X | | X | X | | |
| **Employment** | | | | | | | | |
| E-057 | *Population employed* | 1 | X | | X | X | X | X |
| E-058 | *Employment rate* | 1 | X | | X | X | X | X |
| E-059 | *Employment by sector* | 1 | X | | X | X | | X |
| E-060 | *Employment by class* | 1 | X | | X | X | | X |
| E-061 | *Employment by industry* | 1 | X | | X | X | | X |
| E-062 | *Employment by occupation* | 1 | X | | X | X | | X |
| E-063 | *Distribution of employment by sector* | 1 | X | | X | X | | X |
| E-064 | *Distribution of employment by class* | 1 | X | | X | X | | X |
| E-065 | *Distribution of employment by industry* | 1 | X | | X | X | | X |
| E-066 | *Distribution of employment by occupation* | 1 | X | | X | X | | X |
| E-067 | *Average usual hours of work* | 1 | X | | X | X | | X |
| E-068 | *Average actual and overtime hours of work* | 1 | X | | X | X | | X |
| E-069 | *Average monthly salary* | 1 | X | | X | X | | X |
| **Unemployment** | | | | | | | | |
| E-070 | *Population unemployed* | 1 | X | | X | X | X | X |
| E-071 | Unemployment rate | 1 | X | | X | X | X | X |
| E-072 | Unemployed who have never been employed before | 1 | X | | X | X | | X |
| E-073 | Unemployed who haven been employed before | 1 | X | | X | X | | X |
| E-074 | *Population of discouraged workers* | 1 | X | | X | X | X | X |
| E-075 | *Incidence of discouraged workers* | 1 | X | | X | X | X | X |

## Table 3.3—Summary List of Indicators by QSCFA Goals

| Code / Indicator | | Priority | Family well-being Goal 1–3 | Charters on family affairs Goal 4 | Women's empower-ment Goal 5 | Women's work Goal 6 | Support those with special needs Goal 7 | Youth challenges Goal 9 |
|---|---|---|---|---|---|---|---|---|
| | | | | Family Life | | | | |
| **Household structure and composition** | | | | | | | | |
| F-001 | *Total number of households* | 1 | X | | X | | | |
| F-002 | Total household distribution | 1 | X | | X | | | X |
| F-003 | Average household size | 1 | X | | X | | | X |
| F-004 | *Orphaned children* | 1 | X | | X | | | X |
| **Marriage and divorce** | | | | | | | | |
| F-005 | Crude marriage rate | 1 | X | | X | | | X |
| F-006 | Crude divorce rate | 1 | X | | X | | | X |
| F-007 | Average age at time of first marriage | 1 | X | | X | | | X |
| F-008 | Population who are never married | 1 | X | | X | | | X |
| F-009 | Population who are married | 1 | X | | X | | | X |
| F-010 | *Population who are in polygamous marriages* | 1 | X | | X | | | X |
| F-011 | Population who are seprated | 1 | X | | X | | | X |
| F-012 | Population who are divorced | 1 | X | | X | | | X |
| F-013 | Population who are widowed | 1 | X | | X | | | X |
| **Housing characteristics** | | | | | | | | |
| F-014 | *Distribution of households by tenure (rent, own)* | 1 | X | | X | | | X |
| F-015 | Residential buildings that are connected to the general water grid | 1 | X | | | | | |
| F-016 | Residential buildings that are connected to the sewage system networks | 1 | X | | | | | |
| F-017 | Residential buildings that are connected to the public electricity network | 1 | X | | | | | |
| F-018 | Subsisting households that have a bathroom inside the house | 1 | X | | | | | |
| F-019 | Subsisting households that use gas in the kitchen | 1 | X | | | | | |
| **Poverty** | | | | | | | | |
| F-020 | Population living below the national poverty line | 1 | X | X | X | | X | X |
| F-021 | Poverty gap ratio | 2 | X | X | X | | | |
| F-022 | *Human Poverty Index (HPI-2)* | 2 | X | | X | | | |

65

**Table 3.3—Summary List of Indicators by QSCFA Goals**

| Code / Indicator | | Priority | Family well-being | Charters on family affairs | Women's empower-ment | Women's work | Support those with special needs | Youth challenges |
|---|---|---|---|---|---|---|---|---|
| | | | Goal 1–3 | Goal 4 | Goal 5 | Goal 6 | Goal 7 | Goal 9 |
| **Income** | | | | | | | | |
| F-023 | Female estimated earned income | 2 | X | | X | | | |
| F-024 | Male estimated earned income | 2 | X | | X | | | |
| F-025 | Female earned income relative to male earned income | 2 | X | | X | | | |
| F-026 | Share of income or consumption—Poorest 10% | 2 | X | | X | | | |
| F-027 | Share of income or consumption—Poorest 20% | 2 | X | | X | | | |
| F-028 | Share of income or consumption—Richest 10% | 2 | X | | X | | | |
| F-029 | Share of income or consumption—Richest 20% | 2 | X | | X | | | |
| F-030 | Ratio of richest 10% to poorest 10% | 2 | X | | X | | | |
| F-031 | Ratio of richest 20% to poorest 20% | 2 | X | | X | | | |
| F-032 | Gini index | 2 | X | | X | | | |
| F-033 | Share of household income from female earnings | 2 | X | | X | | | |
| F-034 | Share of household income from male earnings | 2 | X | | X | | | |
| F-035 | Average household monthly income | 1 | X | | X | | | |
| F-036 | Average household monthly income of persons | 1 | X | | X | | | |
| F-037 | Percentage of the population who do not have any source of living | 2 | X | | X | | | |
| F-038 | *Average household debt* | 2 | X | | X | | | |
| **Consumption** | | | | | | | | |
| F-039 | Average monthly household consumption | 2 | X | | X | | | |
| F-040 | Average monthly per capita household consumption | 1 | X | | X | | | |
| F-041 | Household consumer units | 1 | X | | X | | | |
| **Social support** | | | | | | | | |
| F-042 | *Beneficiaries of Zakat* | 2 | X | | X | | | |
| F-043 | Beneficiaries of private or public financial aid | 2 | X | | X | | | |
| F-044 | Beneficiaries of social security | 2 | X | | X | | | |
| F-045 | Elderly in care centers | 2 | X | | | | | |
| F-046 | Beneficiaries of population-support | 2 | X | | | | | |
| F-047 | Population who benefit from health insurance | 2 | X | | | | | |
| F-048 | Beneficiaries of pensions | 2 | X | | | | | |

66

## Table 3.3—Summary List of Indicators by QSCFA Goals

| Code / Indicator | Priority | Family well-being<br>Goal 1–3 | Charters on family affairs<br>Goal 4 | Women's empower-ment<br>Goal 5 | Women's work<br>Goal 6 | Support those with special needs<br>Goal 7 | Youth challenges<br>Goal 9 |
|---|---|---|---|---|---|---|---|
| | | | | Education | | | |
| **Illiteracy** | | | | | | | |
| ED-001 Illiteracy rate | 1 | X | X | X | | X | X |
| **Education enrollment** | | | | | | | |
| ED-002 Enrollment in early-childhood education or early-childhood development programs | 2 | X | | | | X | |
| ED-003 Gross enrollment rates at the primary, secondary, and higher-education levels | 1 | X | X | | | X | X |
| ED-004 *Net enrollment rates at the primary, secondary and higher education levels* | 1 | X | X | | | X | X |
| ED-005 Orphan to non-orphan school enrollment rates | 2 | X | | | | | X |
| ED-006 Students in private K–12 schools | 1 | X | | | | X | X |
| ED-007 Students in public K–12 schools | 1 | X | | | | X | X |
| ED-008 *Students abroad in K–12 schools* | 1 | X | | | | X | X |
| ED-009 Students in universities | 1 | X | | | | X | X |
| ED-010 Students abroad in college on scholarship | 1 | X | | | | X | X |
| ED-011 *Students abroad in college on family support* | 1 | X | | | | X | X |
| ED-012 Students in post-graduate studies | 1 | X | | | | X | X |
| ED-013 *Students abroad in post-graduate studies* | 1 | X | | | | X | X |
| ED-014 Students in special education schools | 1 | X | | | | X | |
| ED-015 Students in Al-Noor Institute | 1 | X | | | | X | |
| ED-016 Students in adult literacy centers and night schools | 1 | X | | | | | |
| ED-017 Students age 65+ in adult literacy centers and night schools | 1 | X | | | | | |
| **Educational attainment** | | | | | | | |
| ED-018 *Educational attainment of the population by years or level* | 1 | X | | X | X | X | X |
| ED-019 *High school graduates* | 1 | X | | X | X | X | X |
| ED-020 *University graduates* | 1 | X | | X | X | X | X |
| ED-021 Children who reach grade 5 | 2 | X | | X | X | X | |
| ED-022 *Rate of grade repetition* | 2 | X | | X | X | X | |
| ED-023 Failure rate in secondary education | 2 | X | | X | X | X | X |
| ED-024 Benefit rate from the merger project for disabled | 2 | | | | | X | |

Table 3.3—Summary List of Indicators by QSCFA Goals

| Code / Indicator | | Priority | Family well-being | Charters on family affairs | Women's empower-ment | Women's work | Support those with special needs | Youth challenges |
|---|---|---|---|---|---|---|---|---|
| | | | Goal 1–3 | Goal 4 | Goal 5 | Goal 6 | Goal 7 | Goal 9 |
| **Training** | | | | | | | | |
| ED-025 | Trainees in the Institute of Administrative Development | 2 | X | | X | X | X | X |
| ED-026 | Trainees in the Languages Center | 2 | X | | X | X | | X |
| ED-027 | Students enrolled in vocational training centers | 1 | X | | X | X | | X |
| **Education expenditures and financing** | | | | | | | | |
| ED-028 | Public expenditure on pre-primary and primary education | 1 | X | | X | | | X |
| ED-029 | Public expenditure on secondary education | 1 | X | | X | | | X |
| ED-030 | Public expenditure on tertiary education | 1 | X | | X | | | X |
| ED-031 | Public expenditure on education as share of GDP | 1 | X | | X | | | X |
| ED-032 | Share of government spending on public education | 1 | X | | X | | | X |
| ED-033 | *Education expenditures per pupil, total and by type* | 1 | X | | X | | | X |
| ED-034 | *Fellowships for higher education by level and specialty* | 2 | X | | X | | | X |
| ***Education expenditures on R&D*** | | | | | | | | |
| ED-035 | *Share of education expenditure for R&D* | 2 | X | | X | | | X |
| ED-036 | *Share of education expenditure for data and networking* | 2 | X | | X | | | X |
| ED-037 | *Education expenditure on R&D as a share of GDP* | 2 | X | | X | | | X |
| **Education index** | | | | | | | | |
| ED-038 | Education index | 1 | X | | X | | | X |
| **Educational services** | | | | | | | | |
| ED-039 | *Public schools* | 1 | X | | | | X | X |
| ED-040 | *Private schools* | 1 | X | | | | X | X |
| ED-041 | Adult literacy centers and night schools | 2 | X | | | | | X |
| ED-042 | Special education schools | 2 | X | | | | X | X |
| ED-043 | *Vocational training centers* | 2 | X | | | | X | X |
| ED-044 | Universities | 1 | X | | | | X | X |
| ED-045 | Teaching staff in schools | 1 | X | | X | X | X | X |
| ED-046 | Administrative staff in schools | 1 | X | | X | X | X | X |
| ED-047 | University faculty | 1 | X | | X | X | X | X |
| ED-048 | *Teacher:pupil ratio* | 2 | X | | X | X | X | X |

## Table 3.3—Summary List of Indicators by QSCFA Goals

| Code / Indicator | | Priority | Family well-being Goal 1–3 | Charters on family affairs Goal 4 | Women's empower-ment Goal 5 | Women's work Goal 6 | Support those with special needs Goal 7 | Youth challenges Goal 9 |
|---|---|---|---|---|---|---|---|---|
| | | | Health and Nutrition | | | | | |
| *Health infrastructure conditions* | | | | | | | | |
| HN-001 | Population with sustainable access to improved water sources | 2 | X | X | | | | |
| HN-002 | Population with access to improved sanitation utilities | 2 | X | X | | | | |
| HN-003 | Population with sustainable access to affordable essential drugs | 2 | X | X | | | | |
| *Health services infrastructure* | | | | | | | | |
| HN-004 | Public hospitals | 1 | X | | | | | |
| HN-005 | Public hospital beds | 1 | X | | | | | |
| HN-006 | Private hospitals | 1 | X | | | | | |
| HN-007 | Public health centers | 1 | X | | | | | |
| HN-008 | Outpatient clinics that are subsidiary to Hamad Medical Corporation | 1 | X | | | | | |
| HN-009 | Armed Forces clinics | 1 | X | | | | | |
| HN-010 | Police clinics | 1 | X | | | | | |
| HN-011 | Qatar Petroleum clinics | 1 | X | | | | | |
| HN-012 | Private clinics and medical complexes | 1 | X | | | | | |
| HN-013 | Governmental primary healthcare units | 1 | X | | | | | |
| HN-014 | Medical centers for athletes | 1 | X | | | | | X |
| HN-015 | Specialized centers for the treatment and rehabilitation of drug addicts | 1 | X | | | | | X |
| HN-016 | Psychotherapy centers | 1 | X | | | | | X |
| HN-017 | Psychological counseling centers | 1 | X | | | | | X |
| HN-018 | Physicians | 1 | X | | | | | |
| HN-019 | Dentists | 1 | X | | | | | |
| HN-020 | Nurses | 1 | X | | | | | |
| HN-021 | Pharmacists | 1 | X | | | | | |
| HN-022 | Other health care providers | 1 | X | | | | | |

Table 3.3—Summary List of Indicators by QSCFA Goals

| Code / Indicator | | Priority | Family well-being Goal 1–3 | Charters on family affairs Goal 4 | Women's empower-ment Goal 5 | Women's work Goal 6 | Support those with special needs Goal 7 | Youth challenges Goal 9 |
|---|---|---|---|---|---|---|---|---|
| *Health services utilization* | | | | | | | | |
| HN-023 | Population who receive health services | 2 | X | | X | | X | X |
| HN-024 | Enrollees in psychological rehabilitation programs | 2 | X | | X | | X | X |
| HN-025 | Population that receive treatment at governmental hospitals | 2 | X | | X | | X | X |
| HN-026 | Population that receive treatment in private hospitals | 2 | X | | X | | X | X |
| HN-027 | Population that receive treatment abroad | 2 | X | | X | | X | X |
| HN-028 | Population that receive treatment at home | 2 | X | | X | | X | X |
| HN-029 | *Utilization rate of health services for acute conditions* | 1 | X | | X | | X | X |
| HN-030 | Incidence of antenatal care | 1 | X | | X | | | |
| HN-031 | Incidence of attended births | 1 | X | X | X | | | |
| HN-032 | Incidence of post-partum care | 1 | X | | X | | | |
| HN-033 | *Incidence of dental care* | 1 | X | | X | | X | X |
| | | | | | | | | |
| *Preventative health services utilization* | | | | | | | | |
| HN-034 | Children immunized in first year of age | 1 | X | | X | | | |
| HN-035 | *Children fully immunized* | 1 | X | | X | | | |
| HN-036 | Children fully vaccinated against polio | 1 | X | | X | | | |
| HN-037 | *Children partially vaccinated against polio* | 1 | X | | X | | | |
| HN-038 | Children fully vaccinated against DPT | 1 | X | | X | | | |
| HN-039 | *Children partially vaccinated against DPT* | 1 | X | | X | | | |
| HN-040 | Children vaccinated against measles | 1 | X | X | X | | | |
| HN-041 | Children vaccinated against tuberculosis | 1 | X | X | X | | | |
| HN-042 | Children fully vaccinated against hepatitis | 1 | X | | X | | | |
| HN-043 | *Children partially vaccinated against hepatitis* | 1 | X | | X | | | |

Table 3.3—Summary List of Indicators by QSCFA Goals

| Code / Indicator | | Priority | Family well-being Goal 1–3 | Charters on family affairs Goal 4 | Women's empower-ment Goal 5 | Women's work Goal 6 | Support those with special needs Goal 7 | Youth challenges Goal 9 |
|---|---|---|---|---|---|---|---|---|
| Health expenditures | | | | | | | | |
| HN-044 | Expenditure on public health as a percentage of GDP | 1 | X | | | | | |
| HN-045 | Expenditure on private health as a percentage of GDP | 1 | X | | | | | |
| HN-046 | Per capita health expenditure | 1 | X | | | | | |
| HN-047 | *Per capita health expenditure, total and by type* | 1 | X | | | | | |
| HN-048 | *Per capita health expenditure on medicines, total and by type* | 2 | X | | | | | |
| HN-049 | *Per capita health expenditure for special needs population, total and by type* | 2 | X | | | | X | |
| Nutritional status | | | | | | | | |
| HN-050 | Undernourished population | 4 | X | | X | | X | X |
| HN-051 | *Incidence of obesity* | 3 | X | | X | | X | X |
| HN-052 | Infants with low birthweight | 1 | X | | X | | | |
| HN-053 | New mothers' vitamin A consumption | 3 | X | | X | | | |
| HN-054 | Children under age 5 under the appropriate weight for their age (wasting) | 3 | X | | X | | | |
| HN-055 | Children under age 5 under the appropriate height for their age (stunting) | 3 | X | | X | | | |
| HN-056 | Prevalence of breastfeeding | 1 | X | | X | | | |
| HN-057 | Prevalence of exclusive breastfeeding | 1 | X | | X | | | |
| HN-058 | Prevalence of breastfeeding continuation | 1 | X | | X | | | |
| HN-059 | Mean duration of breastfeeding | 1 | X | | X | | | |
| HN-060 | Children's vitamin A consumption | 3 | X | | X | | | |
| Women's reproductive health | | | | | | | | |
| HN-061 | Contraceptive prevalence rate | 1 | X | | X | | | X |
| HN-062 | *Contraceptive prevalence rates by method* | 1 | X | | X | | | X |
| HN-063 | Percentage using condom in the latest high-risk sexual intercourse | 3 | X | | X | | | X |
| HN-064 | Mothers vaccinated against natal polo | 3 | X | | X | | | X |
| HN-065 | Abortion rate | 1 | X | | X | | | X |

71

## Table 3.3—Summary List of Indicators by QSCFA Goals

| Code / Indicator | | Priority | Family well-being<br>Goal 1–3 | Charters on family affairs<br>Goal 4 | Women's empower-ment<br>Goal 5 | Women's work<br>Goal 6 | Support those with special needs<br>Goal 7 | Youth challenges<br>Goal 9 |
|---|---|---|---|---|---|---|---|---|
| *Health behaviors* | | | | | | | | |
| HN-066 | Iodine-treated salt consumption per capita | 3 | X | | X | | X | X |
| HN-067 | Cigarette consumption per capita | 2 | X | | X | | X | X |
| HN-068 | *Smoking prevalence* | 1 | X | | X | | | |
| HN-069 | *Drug use prevalence* | 3 | X | | X | | | X |
| HN-070 | *Drug treatment rate* | 3 | X | | X | | | X |
| *Domestic violence* | | | | | | | | |
| HN-071 | *Abuse cases reported by type* | 2 | X | | X | | | |
| Diseases | | | | | | | | |
| HN-072 | Incidence of measles cases | 1 | X | | X | | | X |
| HN-073 | Incidence of  polio cases | 1 | X | | X | | | X |
| HN-074 | Incidence of  malaria cases | 2 | X | | X | | | X |
| HN-075 | Incidence of  tuberculosis cases | 1 | X | | X | | | X |
| HN-076 | Tuberculosis cases detected under DOTS (directly observed treatment, short course) | 2 | X | | X | | | X |
| HN-077 | Tuberculosis cases cured under DOTS | 2 | X | | X | | | X |
| HN-078 | Incidence of low level of urinary iodine | 3 | X | | X | | | X |
| HN-079 | Incidence of diarrhea in children | 2 | X | | X | | | |
| HN-080 | Incidence of tetanus in newborns | 2 | X | | X | | | |
| HN-081 | Incidence of night blindness in children | 2 | X | | X | | | |
| HN-082 | Incidence of inflation of the thyroid in children | 2 | X | | X | | | |
| HN-083 | Children under age 5 ill with fever in 2 weeks prior to survey and treated with anti-malaria drugs | 4 | X | | X | | | |
| HN-084 | Children under age 5 sleeping under insecticide-treated bed nets | 4 | X | | X | | | |
| HN-085 | Incidence of vitamin A deficiency in children | 2 | X | | X | | | |
| HN-086 | Incidence of HIV / AIDS | 1 | X | | X | | | X |
| HN-087 | Incidence of HIV / AIDS in pregnant women | 1 | X | | X | | | |
| HN-088 | Incidence of night blindness in pregnant women | 2 | X | | X | | | |

## Table 3.3—Summary List of Indicators by QSCFA Goals

| Code / Indicator | | Priority | Family well-being<br>Goal 1–3 | Charters on family affairs<br>Goal 4 | Women's empower-ment<br>Goal 5 | Women's work<br>Goal 6 | Support those with special needs<br>Goal 7 | Youth challenges<br>Goal 9 |
|---|---|---|---|---|---|---|---|---|
| HN-089 | Incidence of anemia in pregnant women | 2 | X | | X | | | |
| HN-090 | *Incidence of diarrhea* | 1 | X | | X | | | X |
| HN-091 | *Incidence of high blood pressure* | 1 | X | | X | | | X |
| HN-092 | *Incidence of heart disease* | 1 | X | | X | | | X |
| HN-093 | *Incidence of cancer* | 1 | X | | X | | | X |
| HN-094 | *Incidence of diabetes* | 1 | X | | X | | | X |
| HN-095 | *Rate of diabetics using insulin* | 1 | X | | X | | | X |
| HN-096 | *Incidence of asthma* | 1 | X | | X | | | X |
| HN-097 | Incidence of chronic geriatric diseases | 2 | X | | X | | | X |
| HN-098 | Incidence of physical disabilities | 1 | | | | | X | |
| HN-099 | Incidence of mental disabilities | 1 | | | | | X | |
| *Special needs services* | | | | | | | | |
| HN-100 | Employment at special needs centers | 1 | | | | | X | |
| HN-101 | Employment at Al-Noor Institute | 1 | | | | | X | |
| HN-102 | Faculty in special education schools | 1 | | | | | X | |
| HN-103 | Health care utilization for special needs population | 1 | | | | | X | |
| HN-104 | Residents in hospitals, special needs | 1 | | | | | X | |
| HN-105 | Physical therapy, special needs | 1 | | | | | X | |
| HN-106 | Occupational therapy, special needs | 1 | | | | | X | |
| HN-107 | Rehabilitation treatment, special needs | 1 | | | | | X | |

Table 3.3—Summary List of Indicators by QSCFA Goals

| Code / Indicator | | Priority | Family well-being Goal 1–3 | Charters on family affairs Goal 4 | Women's empower-ment Goal 5 | Women's work Goal 6 | Support those with special needs Goal 7 | Youth challenges Goal 9 |
|---|---|---|---|---|---|---|---|---|
| **Environment** | | | | | | | | |
| *Geography of the state* | | | | | | | | |
| EV-001 | Land area covered by forests | 3 | X | | | | | |
| EV-002 | *Rate of land desertification* | 3 | X | | | | | |
| EV-003 | Protected land area | 3 | X | | | | | |
| *Air* | | | | | | | | |
| EV-004 | Carbon dioxide emissions per capita | 3 | X | | | | | |
| EV-005 | Share of world carbon dioxide emissions | 3 | X | | | | | |
| EV-006 | Consumption of ozone-depleting chlorofluorocarbons | 3 | X | | | | | |
| *Water* | | | | | | | | |
| EV-007 | *Water production by type (extraction, desalination)* | 2 | X | | | | | |
| EV-008 | *Seashore pollution* | 3 | X | | | | | |
| *Energy* | | | | | | | | |
| EV-009 | Electricity consumption per capita | 2 | X | | | | | |
| EV-010 | Share of energy consumption in traditional fuels | 2 | X | | | | | |
| EV-011 | GDP per unit of energy use | 3 | X | | | | | |
| **Civil and Political Life** | | | | | | | | |
| *Cultural activities* | | | | | | | | |
| C-001 | Public libraries | 1 | X | | | | | X |
| C-002 | Newspapers | 1 | X | | | | | X |
| C-003 | Monthly magazines | 1 | X | | | | | X |
| C-004 | Movie theaters | 1 | X | | | | | X |
| C-005 | Clubs, associations, and cooperatives | 1 | X | | | | | X |
| C-006 | Social and cultural clubs | 1 | X | | | | | X |
| C-007 | Scientific clubs | 1 | X | | | | | X |
| C-008 | *Women's associations and unions* | 1 | X | | X | X | | |
| C-009 | Disabled people participating in cultural activities | 1 | | | | | X | |
| C-010 | Youth participating in non-sport activities | 1 | | | | | | X |
| C-011 | Youth establishments | 1 | | | | | | X |

## Table 3.3—Summary List of Indicators by QSCFA Goals

| Code / Indicator | | Priority | Family well-being<br>Goal 1–3 | Charters on family affairs<br>Goal 4 | Women's empower-ment<br>Goal 5 | Women's work<br>Goal 6 | Support those with special needs<br>Goal 7 | Youth challenges<br>Goal 9 |
|---|---|---|---|---|---|---|---|---|
| C-012 | Youth centers | 1 | | | | | | X |
| C-013 | Youth centers associations | 1 | | | | | | X |
| Athletic activities | | | | | | | | |
| C-014 | Players registered in sports clubs | 1 | | | | | | X |
| C-015 | Sports clubs | 1 | | | | | | X |
| C-016 | Sports unions | 1 | | | | | | X |
| C-017 | Sports clubs and societies | 1 | | | | | | X |
| Women's political participation | | | | | | | | |
| C-018 | Women's share of eligible voters in municipal council election | 1 | | | X | | | X |
| C-019 | Women's share of voters for municipal council election | 1 | | | X | | | X |
| C-020 | Women candidates for municipal council | 1 | | | X | | | X |
| C-021 | Women elected to municipal council | 1 | | | X | | | X |
| C-022 | Year women received right to vote | 1 | | | X | | | X |
| C-023 | Year women received right to stand for election | 1 | | | X | | | X |
| C-024 | Year the first woman was elected or appointed as member of parliament | 1 | | | X | | | X |
| C-025 | Women's share of parliamentary seats in lower or single house | 1 | | | X | | | X |
| C-026 | Women's share of parliamentary seats in upper house or senate | 1 | | | X | | | X |
| C-027 | Women's share of government ministerial positions | 1 | | | X | | | X |
| C-028 | Women's share of employment in NGOs | 1 | | | X | | | X |
| C-029 | *Women's share of managers in public and private institutions* | 1 | | | X | | | X |
| **Safety and Security** | | | | | | | | |
| National security | | | | | | | | |
| SS-001 | Total of armed forces | 3 | X | | | | | |
| SS-002 | Conventional arms imports | 3 | X | | | | | |
| SS-003 | Conventional arms exports | 4 | X | | | | | |
| National security expenditures | | | | | | | | |
| SS-004 | Military expenditures | 4 | X | | | | | |

75

## Table 3.3—Summary List of Indicators by QSCFA Goals

| Code / Indicator | | Priority | Family well-being Goal 1–3 | Charters on family affairs Goal 4 | Women's empower-ment Goal 5 | Women's work Goal 6 | Support those with special needs Goal 7 | Youth challenges Goal 9 |
|---|---|---|---|---|---|---|---|---|
| **Crime** | | | | | | | | |
| SS-005 | *Homicide rate* | 2 | X | | X | | X | X |
| SS-006 | *Crime victimization rates* | 2 | X | | X | | X | X |
| SS-007 | *Rate of juvenile delinquency* | 1 | | | | | | X |
| SS-008 | *Drug share of illegal seizures* | 2 | X | | | | | X |
| SS-009 | *Drug share of convictions* | 2 | X | | | | | X |
| **Accidents** | | | | | | | | |
| SS-010 | *Automobile accidents* | 1 | X | | | | | X |
| SS-011 | *Fatal automobile accidents* | 1 | X | | | | | X |
| SS-012 | *Automobile accident fatalities* | 1 | X | | | | | X |
| SS-013 | *Youth share of automobile accidents* | 1 | X | | | | | X |
| SS-014 | *Youth share of fatal automobile accidents* | 1 | X | | | | | X |
| SS-015 | *Youth share of automobile accident fatalities* | 1 | X | | | | | X |
| **Immigration** | | | | | | | | |
| SS-016 | Women's share among immigrants | 2 | X | | X | | | |
| SS-017 | Women's share among emigrants | 2 | X | | X | | | |
| **Refugees** | | | | | | | | |
| SS-018 | Internally displaced persons | 4 | X | | | | | |
| SS-019 | Refugees by country of asylum | 4 | X | | | | | |
| SS-020 | Refugees by country of origin | 4 | X | | | | | |
| | | | Statutory | | | | | |
| **Conventions** | | | | | | | | |
| ST-001 | International Convention on the Elimination of All Forms of Racial Discrimination, 1965 | 1 | X | X | | | | |
| ST-002 | International Covenant on Civil and Political Rights, 1966 | 1 | X | X | | | | |
| ST-003 | International Covenant on Economic, Social and Cultural Rights, 1966 | 1 | X | X | | | | |
| ST-004 | Convention of Elimination of All Forms of Discrimination Against Women, 1979 | 1 | X | X | X | X | | |

## Table 3.3—Summary List of Indicators by QSCFA Goals

| Code / Indicator | | Priority | Family well-being Goal 1–3 | Charters on family affairs Goal 4 | Women's empower-ment Goal 5 | Women's work Goal 6 | Support those with special needs Goal 7 | Youth challenges Goal 9 |
|---|---|---|---|---|---|---|---|---|
| ST-005 | Convention Against Torture and Other Cruel, Inhuman or Degrading Treatment or Punishment, 1984 | 1 | X | X | | | | |
| ST-006 | Convention on Rights of the Child, 1989 | 1 | X | X | | | | |
| ST-007 | International Convention on the Rights of Persons with Disabilities | 1 | | | | | X | |
| Labor rights conventions | | | | | | | | |
| ST-008 | Freedom of association and collective bargaining—Convention 98 | 1 | X | X | X | X | | |
| ST-009 | Elimination of forced and compulsory labor—Convention 29 | 1 | X | X | X | X | | |
| ST-010 | Elimination of discrimination in respect of employment and occupation—Convention 111 | 1 | X | X | X | X | X | |
| ST-011 | Abolishing child labor—Conventions 138 and 182 | 1 | X | X | | | | X |
| Ratification of environmental treaties | | | | | | | | |
| ST-0012 | Cartagena Protocol on Biosafety, 2000 | 1 | X | X | | | | |
| ST-0013 | Framework Convention on Climate Change, 1992 | 1 | X | X | | | | |
| ST-0014 | Kyoto Protocol to the Framework Convention on Climate Change, 1997 | 1 | X | X | | | | |
| ST-0015 | Convention on Biological Diversity, 1992 | 1 | X | X | | | | |

NOTES: For list of QSCFA goals, see Table 1.1 in Chapter One. Indicators or units of measurement that were not listed in the QSCFA prototype database as of March 2004 are shown in italics. Priority scale ranking is from 1 (highest) to 4 (lowest).

# 4. QSCFA Database Architecture

In this chapter, we discuss the current prototype database architecture and its strengths and limitations with respect to supporting the current and future goals of the QSCFA for a social indicators database system. We propose possible strategies to address the limitations we identify.

## The Prototype Database

As seen in Figure 4.1, the prototype social indicators database is implemented in Lotus Notes/Domino, version 6.x. Lotus Notes/Domino is a "groupware" software package, designed to facilitate sharing and collaboration across an organization through integrated email, calendaring, database, and Web content creation facility. This software platform allows a great deal of flexibility in the contents of individual records in a database. It also allows for a systematic structure in cataloging the individual records. The prototype, as currently implemented, takes advantage of both of these features.

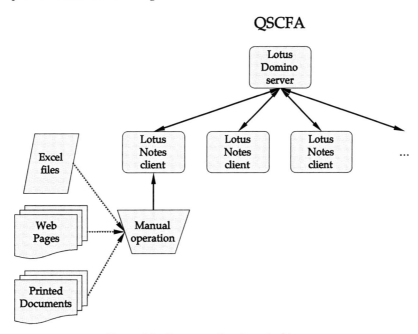

Figure 4.1—Prototype Database Architecture

Lotus Notes/Domino was chosen as the software platform for implementation of the prototype for three reasons. The first is that the information technology staff of the QSCFA were familiar with Lotus Notes/Domino. The second reason is that Lotus Notes/Domino was already being used within the QSCFA for email and calendaring, and it seemed reasonable to try to develop a system on a software platform with which the general QSCFA staff had some familiarity. The third reason is that Lotus Notes/Domino lends itself to rapid prototyping of simple databases; developing a basic data hierarchy and user interface to the data is very simple.

## Database Structure (Storage)

Individual records include both data and metadata documenting the data. The data generally consist of a time series of a given indicator. Sometimes a single record will contain multiple time series (e.g., Qatari, Non-Qatari, Total) for a given indicator; these are generally sorted by year, then by subcategory. The structure is sufficiently flexible to allow storage of data elements from different sources for what is nominally the same measure; this is useful when there are marked differences between multiple sources for the "same" indicator. The metadata included in the record documents the source and sometimes the algorithm used to compute a derived indicator; for example, some indicators contain a link to an Excel spreadsheet that contains either the raw data or the computation for a derived indicator. Occasionally, a record will consist of a document pertaining to the contents of many other records, e.g., the Child's Rights Convention is stored as a record in the database.

Time series are typically rendered as a percentage of the relevant population, though other renderings are used as appropriate (e.g., infant mortality rate is rendered as per 1,000 living births). The individual observations are recorded to the published precision. This results in some precision loss over storing the numerator and the denominator of the relevant statistic, which would allow for computing the summary statistic (for example, a percentage) to arbitrary precision. This also precludes directly answering some elementary data analysis questions—that is, if a percentage figure is rising, is it rising due to a relative increase in the numerator, or a relative decrease in the denominator?

The individual records are stored in a rigidly structured hierarchy. This hierarchy allows for rapid access to indicators relevant to a particular narrow subject area. The top level of the hierarchy (the "group") largely parallels the organization of the QSCFA: Childhood, Youth, Women, Elderly, Disabled, and

Family.[1] The second level of the hierarchy (the "sector") divides the individual records into several categories. For example, the Childhood group is divided into Demography, Education, Health and Nutrition, Labour and Employment, and Statutory sectors. Specific sectors may appear in all groups: for example, Demography or Demographic sectors. Other sectors may appear in one or more, but not all, groups; for example, the Communication and Publicity sector is unique to the Family group. The third level of the hierarchy further divides the individual records into subcategories ("subsector") appropriate to the group and Sector; for example, the Childhood group's Demography sector contains the following subsectors: Population Structure, Population Growth, and Child's Mortality Rate Who are Beneath the Age Five (sic).

## Data Entry

Currently, data are entered manually into the database, largely from publications by the Planning Council, as illustrated in Figure 4.1. There is nothing in the database design to preclude automating data entry, provided data are made available in a machine-readable format, either via magnetic or optical media, or via a local or wide-area network. Standard extensions for Lotus Notes/Domino allow for open database connectivity (ODBC), for example IBM® NotesSQL® allows the use of standard structured query language (SQL) expressions to query and update a Lotus Notes/Domino database file.

## Data Retrieval

It is worth noting at this point that most users within QSCFA have some familiarity with Lotus Notes/Domino, if only through using it for email. Thus, one of the major hurdles encountered in promulgating use of a software package has already been passed: Most potential users of the database already use Lotus Notes/Domino for their daily tasks. Familiarity with basic operations within Lotus Notes/Domino (e.g., cutting and pasting) will translate into familiarity with the basics of operating the database application.

Data retrieval is facilitated by the hierarchical storage system used for the individual records. A user may view an individual record and the associated metadata. A user may also customize views to examine multiple individual records simultaneously. Simple printed reports or graphs can be generated from

---

[1] Where the original label in the database is in Arabic, we use the English translation as provided by the QSCFA.

an individual record. A user can copy either the whole record or selected elements of the record and paste these data into another package (e.g., Microsoft Excel) for further data manipulation.

## Data Manipulation

Lotus Notes/Domino supports two languages for manipulating data. An applications programmer can use either the "formula" language, which is reminiscent of the formulas used in spreadsheet programs such as IBM® Lotus® 1-2-3® or Microsoft Excel, or an applications programmer can use a "scripting" language that is similar to structured BASIC. Both of these languages require some expertise in the particulars of the programming environment of Lotus Notes/Domino. The facilities offered by the scripting language in particular allow for almost any conceivable manipulation of data, limited only by the imagination and the skill of the individual programmer. However, the amount of labor associated with programming data manipulation tasks would be greater than the amount of labor needed to accomplish similar tasks in a higher-level language specifically oriented toward data manipulation, such as SQL.

It is worth noting that the free-form nature of the individual records would make a programmer's job more difficult than if the records were rigidly structured. A great deal of code would have to be written merely to ensure retrieval of the correct data element from within an individual record, before any further manipulation would take place.

In practice, if a user requires anything beyond the most basic data retrieval, the user would likely copy data from an individual record in the database, paste it into a spreadsheet package such as Microsoft Excel, and use Excel's data manipulation facilities for further data processing.

# Strengths and Limitations of the Prototype Database

This section gives a brief assessment of the strengths and limitations of the prototype database. We find that some elements that are strengths within one context can in turn be weaknesses within another context. This assessment will inform our discussion of strategies for addressing the limitations of the prototype database.

*Strengths*

The strengths of the prototype database are manifold. Primary among them is the fact that the potential user base is already familiar with the basics of operating the database software. In addition, the strict hierarchical organization of the individual records, along with the nearly free-form nature of the individual records themselves, provides a powerful combination of abilities that is hard to beat. Furthermore, the database and the software platform it is based on are sufficiently flexible and extensible enough to take on nearly any task. We will discuss each of these strengths in turn.

**User-base familiarity.** As noted above, the potential user base within the QSCFA uses Lotus Notes/Domino on a daily basis for email, calendaring, and other activities. This familiarity with Lotus Notes/Domino will translate into familiarity with the basics of using the social indicators database. This strength is difficult to overestimate; the barriers encountered in getting a community of busy professionals to familiarize themselves with a new software package can be considerable. The ability to access the data within the same package used for the collaborative activity that will be based on assessments of the data is quite useful.

**Strict hierarchical organization.** The individual time series are stored within a strict hierarchy that broadly parallels the organization of the QSFCA itself. This organization allows individual departments to readily access the data pertinent to their areas of responsibility without being distracted by irrelevant measures. The organization is clear and precise, and facilitates both locating existing data and determining if a particular data element is not to be found in the dataset.

**Flexibility in individual record format.** As noted above, Lotus Notes/Domino allows considerable flexibility in the format of individual records. This is good in that it allows storage of metadata, or "data about data," in addition to the data elements themselves. All too often, the sole documentation for a data element in a particular database is an eight-character variable name, or, in more comprehensive databases, a one-line description of the data element. The flexibility of the record format in Lotus Notes/Domino allows and even encourages more complete documentation of individual data elements. This type of documentation is essential to understanding what individual indicators mean and what valid inferences can be drawn from a particular indicator.

**Extensibility.** The Lotus Notes/Domino scripting language, in the hands of a skillful programmer, is capable of performing nearly any data manipulation task. In addition, extension packages to provide connectivity to databases, report writing, and graphics are readily available.

## *Limitations*

Sometimes, what is considered a strength in one context can be a weakness in another. Two of the limitations we highlight below, *strict hierarchical organization* and *flexibility in individual record format*, fall into this category. Such limitations are almost inevitable when designing any software application; it is nearly impossible to design a database to be all things to all individuals. On the whole, though, we find that the disadvantages of these two characteristics outweigh the advantages.

**Manual data entry.** The data in the current prototype are entered manually. Data are typed in from published reports or copied manually from Web pages or Excel spreadsheets. Manually updating the database is an onerous and lengthy task that can be prone to error. Numbers can be entered incorrectly, the wrong cell can be copied from a spreadsheet, and so on. Ensuring that the data are entered accurately and reflect the source publications, Web pages, and Excel spreadsheets is difficult and time-consuming.

**Strict hierarchical organization.** The strict hierarchical organization of the database is a distinct advantage in locating individual records pertinent to a particular department, e.g., Childhood. However, this can make it difficult to compare thematically similar statistics across groups. For example, indicators bearing on population structure and growth are distributed across six groups: Childhood, Youth, Women, Elderly, Special Needs, and Family. While in theory a customized view might be developed so that statistics could be compared across groups, in practice it is more likely that it would be easier to copy the relevant records from the database and paste them into another application for further manipulation and study.

**Flexibility in individual record format.** This is a two-edged sword. While the flexibility in the format of individual records allows for storage of multiple time series, alternate time series (if a second data source is available), and metadata to document the time series, it also means that an individual record can contain nearly anything. This can make it very difficult to design an algorithm to automate data processing. As it stands, the flexibility is put to good use in providing a complete and well-documented source of data, but manipulation of the data within the database would either call on human intervention or demand great ingenuity on the part of a programmer.

**Difficulty in performing computations.** The unstructured nature of individual records leads to difficulty in performing computations. While this has not been an issue up until now, this may become an issue in the near future as the mission of the QSCFA leads to a demand for more sophisticated and precise measures. "Applications requiring complex queries or statistical calculations are not appropriate for Lotus Notes" (Thomas and Peasley, 1998, p. 14).

## Assessment of the Prototype Database System Capabilities

In Chapter Two, we identified several uses for a social indicators database system—and the associated database system features—that would fulfill the short-term objectives of the QSCFA. As stated above, the database may be used to track progress in a given domain or for a given outcome, compare alternative measures of a given indicator, examine indicators for population subgroups or geographic areas, and generate statistics for QSCFA reports or for international agency reports. In terms of the desired features, the database needs to be flexible enough to accommodate multiple indicators, store indicators for multiple years, allow indicators to be analyzed as levels or rates, record indicators in aggregate and for disaggregated groups or geographic areas, and allow for the addition of new fields for each indicator over time or the addition of new indicators over time.

In this section, we ask whether the prototype database can support these activities and achieve these features. In answering this question, we consider both the current implementation of the social indicators database, as well as the capabilities inherent in the software platform that hosts the database.

- *Track progress in a given domain or for a given outcome.* Provided that the appropriate measures are available in the database, the system will allow users to track progress in a given domain or for a given outcome. There are some instances in the current implementation of the database, however, where data are organized in a fashion that does not directly facilitate an understanding of the data. For example, a particular record may include observations pertaining to male Qataris, female Qataris, and all Qataris, sorted by year. Thus, the first data element in the record is the value of the indicator for, say, male Qataris in 1990; the second element is the value for female Qataris in 1990; the third element is the total for 1990; the fourth element is the value for male Qataris in 1991; and so on. This organization makes it difficult to ascertain a trend by simply "eyeballing" the data. This type of problem is relatively easy to fix, however, by simply re-sorting the data, first by gender, and then by year.

- *Compare alternative measures of a given indicator.* As noted above, the flexibility of the format of the individual records in the database allows for storage of multiple alternate values for a given indicator for a given year. Thus, potentially multiple time series of the "same" indicator (computed using alternate methodologies, for example) could be available for a user to compare.

- *Examine indicators for population subgroups or geographic areas.* There is no technical bar to this in the database architecture.

- *Generate statistics for QSCFA reports or for international agency reports.* The system allows for the ready retrieval of precomputed measures. While it is relatively simple to print out a given set of measures, automating production of complicated reports may be quite difficult due to the problems noted above in automating the retrieval of data elements.

- *Accommodate multiple indicators.* We find that there is no technical bar to this in the database architecture.

- *Store indicators for multiple years.* Again, there is no technical bar to this in the database architecture.

- *Allow indicators to be analyzed as levels or rates.* Here, again, there is no technical bar to implementing this feature in the database architecture. Currently, data are stored mostly as rates, however this rate data could be supplemented with level data. The relative difficulty of programming Lotus Notes/Domino may tip the balance in favor of storing precomputed rate data rather than computing rates "on the fly" from the level data (that is, not storing the rate but computing the rate on demand from stored numerator and denominator data).

- *Record indicators in aggregate and for disaggregated groups or geographic areas.* This is another feature that the database architecture can support.

- *Add new fields for each indicator over time or add new indicators over time.* Again, there is no technical barrier to implementing this feature given the database architecture.

In Chapter Two, we also identified several other objectives for a database system to fulfill the long-term objectives of the QSCFA. Chief among these is the ability to store and manipulate microdata. While the Lotus Notes/Domino platform is capable of supporting storage of the data, it is not suitable for performing complex data operations or statistical calculations. It is, however, eminently suitable for storing documentation and other supplemental information on microdata files, and for the storage of indicators derived from microdata files.

## Recommendations for the Social Indicators Database System Architecture

This section discusses how the database system could be changed to address the limitations identified above. We also briefly discuss the desirability of adhering to international standards in the coding of particular data elements. A related issue we touch on is the feasibility and desirability of adopting one or more international systems of classification of indicators to facilitate direct access to specific indicators on the part of expert users.

### The Recommended Database System Architecture

Based on these observations regarding the strengths and weaknesses of the existing prototype, we make the following recommendations:

- Establish standards for electronic data exchange.

- Use a dedicated database management system (DBMS) for storage, manipulation, and retrieval of data.

- Adopt a three-tiered client/server database architecture: client, application server or Web server, and database server.

- Implement the database system user interface as a Web browser application using non-proprietary standards, rather than a Lotus Notes/Domino–specific application.

- Add a provision for ad hoc queries.

We briefly review each of these recommendations in turn below; technical details regarding these recommendations are addressed in Appendix A.

**Establish standards for electronic data exchange.** The vast majority of the indicators identified in this report are based on data published by the Planning Council, though other agencies will likely provide data as well. As noted above, such data are currently entered manually. This makes maintenance of the database laborious, time-consuming, and error-prone. Thus, we recommend that the QSCFA establish standards for electronic data exchange with the Planning Council and other agencies. We recommend adopting the non-proprietary XML standard for transmitting machine-readable databases, as XML is becoming the common representation language for document interchange over the Web. This would be in addition to any human-readable electronic provision of data by the Planning Council or other agencies (e.g., via Web pages.)

**Use a dedicated database management system (DBMS) for storage, manipulation, and retrieval of data.** Three of the limitations noted above are largely due to the nature of the software platform used to implement the prototype. While the characteristics of the native database of Lotus Notes/Domino make it a useful platform for creating prototype applications to demonstrate capabilities, these characteristics can lead to difficulty in a production environment. Thus, we recommend adopting a DBMS for the storage and manipulation of data, using either a relational database management system (RDBMS) or a data warehouse.

**Adopt a three-tiered client/server database architecture: client, application server or Web server, and database server.** We recommend adopting a three-tiered client/server architecture to support the use of either the RDBMS or the data warehouse recommended above, and to provide more flexibility and functionality for the end users. The three tiers consist of (1) a client tier, which provides a graphical user interface (GUI) or Web browser; (2) an application server or Web server tier, which provides application programs or Web pages to act as intermediaries between the client and the database server, and can provide for access-control and other security measures; and (3) a database server tier, which provides the database management system. This is rapidly becoming the standard best practice for many Web applications. (The current prototype uses a two-tier architecture, with Lotus Domino serving as both the database and application server, and Lotus Notes as the client.) This three-tiered database architecture is illustrated in Figure 4.2.

**Implement the database system user interface as a Web browser application using non-proprietary standards, rather than a Lotus Notes/Domino–specific application.** This recommendation stems from two factors: (1) the desirability of using non-proprietary standards, and (2) ease of integration with other Web-based resources. Non-proprietary standards are desirable in that they free the database from dependence upon any particular software manufacturer. This will aid in ensuring that the database can be migrated to newer and better environments as the state of the art improves. The ease of integration with other Web-based resources is useful in particular because of the stated intention of the Planning Council to provide a Web-based interface for the QSCFA indicators that it is tasked with producing. Such an interface may also be possible with other

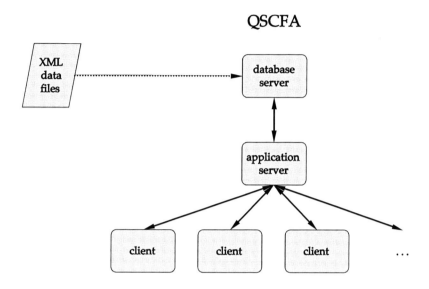

Figure 4.2—Proposed Database Architecture

government ministries or other external sources of data. An example of how such integration might work is illustrated in general in Figure 4.3 for any given external data source, though the initial application is likely to be with the Planning Council.

**Add a provision for ad hoc queries.** The recommended list of indicators in Chapter Three is our best assessment of the indicators that are currently needed by the QSCFA to execute its missions. However, the needs of the QSCFA may change over time, or new data or ways of looking at data may come to light. Thus, we recommend that in addition to providing the listed indicators, the system should provide some mechanism for ad hoc queries. This will give the QSCFA the capability to respond quickly to requests, or handle data "emergencies." This capability will help to ensure that the database system will continue to be relevant into the future.

The capability to generate ad hoc queries will also aid the staff of the QSCFA by enabling them to gain greater insight into the data. They can gain this insight through interactive data analysis, using the system to look at the data in alternate ways to test a hypothesis or to see if there is anything out of the ordinary. This type of interactive data analysis can also be a great aid to quality-assurance; often

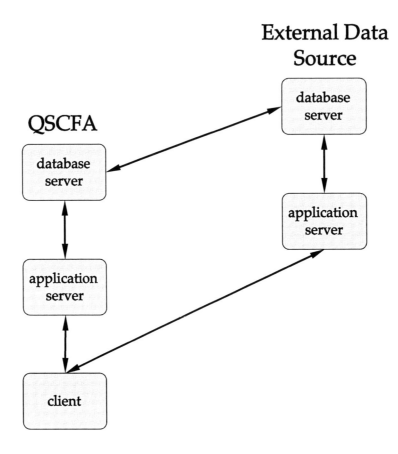

Figure 4.3—Integration with External Data Sources

flaws that cannot be seen in static reports become strikingly apparent given the right tabulation or visualization of the data.

Fortunately, providing the capability to perform ad hoc queries is built into modern database systems. At a minimum, such a capability is provided by query languages such as the SQL language used by most RDBMSs. However, many database systems also provide more "user-friendly" interfaces to allow less sophisticated users to construct arbitrary queries.

### International Coding and Classification Standards

Many international standards exist for coding and classifying economic and social data, such as the System of National Accounts (SNA) or the International

Standard Industrial Classification (ISIC) systems (see United Nations Statistics Division, 1993, 2002). In this section, we will discuss coding and classification standards, and how they might be applied in the context of the indicators database.

**Coding standards.** Some advantages accrue in following international coding standards. Following standards provides some measure of quality-control over the data, and also allows for the comparison of data with the data of other countries that have adopted the same standard. Such standards can also provide a useful guide in specifying valid values an indicator may take.

Some of the elements of the prototype database, such as national income accounts data, have well-established international standards for coding. Others, such as *trainees in the Institute of Administrative Development* (discussed in the Chapter Three), do not have (or need) an associated coding standard. Others may be data elements whose values are provided by agencies outside of Qatar that set the standard, such as the United Nations *Human Development Index*. As a result, the number of elements in the database that are candidates for international standards coding (or recoding) is limited. (Here, we distinguish such coding standards from standard *definitions* of particular indicators, such as the *dependency ratio*.) Aside from indicators that derive from national accounts data, the only indicators for which international coding standards seem applicable are *cause-specific mortality* (for which the International Classification of Disease [ICD], at some level of aggregation, would be appropriate), internationally accepted occupation and industry coding systems, and indicators calculated by the United Nations, such as the HDI.

In many cases, the supporting agency that provides data to the QSCFA may have already adopted an appropriate standard. For example, the Planning Council reports national income accounts data following the SNA standard, and HMC classifies morbidity using ICD. In other cases, the supporting agency may have decided to adapt an existing international system to the special needs of Qatar, such as the commodity classification system used by the Planning Council in reporting foreign-trade data.

In the future, additional measures that are candidates for using some international coding standard may be added to the database. In considering the adoption or promulgation of a coding standard, some thought would need to be given to the following questions:

1.  Is this the most appropriate standard for Qatar?

2.  Is this the best of the competing standards? Is there literature pointing to the superiority of one standard versus another?

3.  What benefit would accrue to the QSCFA if it goes to the effort of recoding existing data or mandating that supporting agencies recode the data they supply?

4.  What information might be lost in the recoding due to differences in the subdivision of data in the international standard versus the data collected?

5.  What information might be lost due to aggregation imposed by the international standard?

**Classification systems.** International classification systems can provide a hierarchical cataloging system, similar to the "call numbers" used to classify books in a library. This can be very useful to expert users who are familiar with the data cataloging system, as they can directly access the data element they need without, for example, having to navigate a menu tree.

Currently, there is no general system for classifying all social indicators. There are classification systems for certain subsets of data, such as for national income accounts. There is a classification scheme used by the United Nations to group human development indicators. But there exists no single scheme that would cover all measures in the QSCFA database. There are also measures, unique to Qatar, that fit into no existing international classification scheme. Thus, the QSCFA would have to largely invent a classification scheme for the data elements in the database of indicators.

In light of this discussion, our recommendation is that, where appropriate, the international standard classification numbers or codes used to refer to a particular indicator be stored in a searchable field of the database. This feature would allow quick access to certain statistics of interest by experts familiar with international classification schemes.

# 5. Conclusions and Recommendations

In support of its mission to ensure strong, healthy, and engaged families in Qatar, the QSCFA has developed a social indicators database system that will be used by the Council's six departments, focusing on the family, women, childhood, youth, the elderly, and people with special needs. Our review of the prototype database indicates that the current database has many strengths, both in terms of the current architecture, as well as the set of indicators planned for inclusion in the database.

We posed four questions in the first chapter relating to the goals of the database system, the database content and indicators, and the database architecture. In this chapter, we summarize our key findings and recommendations, highlighted in earlier chapters, regarding each of these topics. We also draw other implications from these findings and highlight a series of strategic actions for further database implementation to meet both short-term and long-term objectives.

## Database Objectives

As discussed in Chapter Two, the QSCFA social indicators database system may serve both short-term and long-term objectives. Among the short-term objectives, the QSCFA database can be used to track progress over time for a given indicator or group of indicators, compare alternative measures of a given indicator, examine indicators for population subgroups or geographic areas, and generate statistics for various reports. In the short-term, we expect that the QSCFA will draw on other sources of data for the indicators stored in the database.

The social indicators database system also has longer-term potential to meet the ongoing needs of the QSCFA by providing even greater support of analysis, planning, and decisionmaking. In particular, by analyzing the underlying microdata used to generate the summary measures or indicators and/or by collecting and analyzing new data not currently available to support decisionmaking, it would be possible to develop a better understanding of the relationship between indicators and the effects of specific policies.

Our understanding of the short-term and longer-term objectives of the QSCFA leads to the following two recommendations:

- *The QSCFA social indicators database system should be developed with both short-term and long-term goals in mind.* The clear initial focus is on developing a comprehensive, reliable, and accessible database of summary indicators. Future developments would move in the direction of developing the capacity for a database of data that can be used for wider policy analysis. Ideally, decisions made in support of the short-term objectives will be consistent with the longer-term goals as well. Choices in the near-term that might hinder the longer-term objectives should be considered carefully to determine whether other options are available to support both sets of objectives.

- *The QSCFA should eventually develop of a database with detailed information on individuals or families and the physical and human capacity to analyze such data.* This more expansive database will fulfill a longer-term vision for the QSCFA in terms of its mission to formulate effective policies. Meeting this longer-term objective would require the associated physical infrastructure: the ability to store, manipulate, and analyze detailed microdata that already exist or new data that may be collected, and the associated staff expertise; the capacity to design new data collection efforts; and the resources to analyze the resulting data.[1]

## Database Content and Indicators

Given the breadth and depth of the issues facing users of the QSCFA social indicators database system, the subjects covered by the database and the sources of data will be equally comprehensive. The broad subject domains we introduced in Chapter Two and use to organize the detailed indicators in Chapter Three are consistent with the current database structure. Likewise, the fields in the database are consistent with our recommendation to incorporate information on the indicator label and its definition, the population unit, the date of measurement, the unit of measure, the data source, methodological notes, and other fields.

Chapter Three contains a detailed list of 373 indicators recommended for inclusion in the database, along with a definition of each indicator and possible source data. This list reflects indicators currently included in the prototype database, as well as other indicators recommended by the QSCFA departments and research staff as relevant for their objectives. We have also added other indicators that we believe are important for meeting the goals of the QSCFA and

---

[1] The collection of the data may be undertaken by other public or private organizations.

its departments. For many indicators, data readily exist to compute the measure or the indicator is already available through various Qatari government reports or other international reports, such as the UNDP *Human Development Report*.

Given how extensive the list of indicators is, we noted in Chapter Three that it is appropriate to assign a priority ranking to the indicators in order to allocate resources effectively to the collection of the relevant data and the incorporation of the indicators into the database. We have indicated our recommended rankings on a four-point scale. The QSCFA may wish to modify those rankings based on its own assessment of the relative priorities across indicators and the ease of obtaining the necessary data.

## Refining the List of Indicators Over Time

Beyond the recommendations made in Chapter Three, we also note that consideration should be given to the process of refining the database indicators over time. The recommended list of indicators for the database, presented in detail in Chapter Three, is large. It is based on the contents of the current prototype, suggestions of the QSCFA staff, and other relevant indicators we identified. Yet, the list of indicators presented here should not be viewed as static. Indeed, there is an expectation that new indicators we have not covered will be needed in the future, while indicators currently recommended may no longer be required.

The sheer variety of indicators presents a problem for data quality control. Each indicator will have to be updated over time, and the QSCFA will have to exercise some limited responsibility to ensure that the new data received is consistent with earlier data series for each indicator. While some of this process can be automated, human judgment will be an indispensable part of this process.

Due to the limited resources of the QSCFA, it is appropriate that the QSCFA should ensure that it is expending effort to collect and update only those indicators that are truly needed. Thus, we make the following recommendations:

- *Reevaluate the set of indicators on at least an annual basis.* This review should be made first to ensure that all the indicators actively maintained in the database will be required to meet current or future needs of the QSCFA and its departments. Second, the QSCFA should review the set of indicators on at least an annual basis to ensure that all the essential data needs of the Council are being met. While the set of indicators presented in this document reflects the current needs of the QSCFA, in the future, the QSCFA's mission may expand, new sources of data may become available, or new reporting requirements may come forth, and thus new indicators will be required. This process of annual review should be undertaken formally as part of a designated committee of the QSCFA staff, with representation from the various functional and support departments.

- *With indicators that are discontinued, determine the treatment of information stored in the database.* Based on the annual (or more frequent) review, the QSCFA will have identified a set of indicators that are no longer required. Those indicators that are determined to be no longer relevant to the QSCFA's mission can be "deactivated" in one of two ways. The indicator could remain in the database where it is accessible to users in the future but can be designated as "discontinued" in terms of any future updates. This will allow access to historical information in the database, but it should be clear that new information is not being added for the indicator. Alternatively, a deactivated indicator may be dropped from the database so that it is no longer accessible to users. We would recommend archiving the data for those indicators that are removed so that the information can be restored in the future should it be determined to be relevant for the QSCFA at a later point in time.

- *With indicators that are added to the database, determine whether historical information will be stored along with contemporary and future data.* The review of indicators will also identify a set of indicators that should be added to the database. When new indicators are added, it should be determined whether historical information for the indicator will be added along with current and future data. This determination should be made based on available resources, the cost of obtaining historical data, and the needs of the database users.

- *Review the database fields to determine whether new fields are needed, or whether old ones can be discontinued.* The database review can also be used to determine whether all fields in the database for each indicator are needed, and whether there is a need to introduce one or more new fields. Again, we recommend that fields no longer needed be deactivated and archived so the information can be restored if it is required again in the future. New fields that are created may need to be "back-filled" for indicators already in the database or designated as new fields to be used only for new indicators as they are added to the database. The approach used would be based on whether resources are available to obtain the information for existing indicators and the need for such information across the indicators in the database.

- *Communicate to users on a regular basis changes in the database indicators and fields.* Such changes in the database in terms of new or discontinued indicators and fields should be thoroughly documented and communicated to database users on a regular basis so they are aware of changes as they occur. Likewise, other periodic updates to the database or corrections to information in the database should be routinely communicated to users. This information could be conveyed in writing and through a "bulletin board" accessible to users as part of the database interface.

## Measurement of Indicators

There are a number of crucial issues to consider when measuring the various indicators recommended in Chapter Three. We draw on our analysis of the recommended indicators to make several general recommendations regarding indicator measurement:

- *Carefully determine the underlying population for any given indicator so that comparisons over time are consistent.* Given the various subgroups that are often used to measure certain indicators, especially those that are population-based, it is important that the social indicators database system provide a clear indication of the relevant population for a given indicator. For example, is the measure for Qataris, non-Qataris, or both? Was the indicator calculated for people of all ages or for a given age range? Was the indicator calculated only for those who met certain criteria (e.g., those who sought medical treatment, or those who married in the country)? Often, the relevant population can change in subtle ways across surveys due to changes in survey methods over time. In some cases, it may be possible to reconstruct indicators to be defined over a consistent population through time.

- *Record indicators in the database, where relevant and feasible, as both levels and rates.* For some indicators, it is important to determine whether changes in a rate over time are the result of changes in the numerator or changes the denominator or both. When such data are not available, it is important to consider alternative explanations for patterns observed in an indicator over time.

- *Obtain, where possible and relevant, estimates of the standard errors associated with particular indicators.* There may be considerable up-and-down movement of the point-estimates of a particular indicator over time, but such movement may reflect, in part, underlying sampling variability when the indicator is based on sample data or other variables introduced in calculating the indicator. Ideally, standard errors would be available to assess the confidence interval for indicators that are not based on a complete enumeration of the population. This allows for a determination as to whether variation over time in an indicator represents meaningful change or merely statistical variability. Likewise, the significance of differences in an indicator across groups or data sources can be assessed. When such standard errors are not available, changes over time or other differences must be interpreted with caution.

## Database Architecture

We found several strengths in the existing prototype database: It provides a user-friendly platform that the user base already has some familiarity with due to current use of Lotus Notes/Domino in performing daily tasks (e.g., email). Another prominent strength of the current prototype is that it allows considerable flexibility in the storage of data and associated metadata. Finally, and perhaps most importantly, the existing prototype is extensible and thus allows for enhancement and expansion of capability over time.

We also found some limitations in the current database architecture. Manual entry of the data in the current prototype is a key issue, both due to the time-consuming nature of manual entry and the potential for introducing errors. Another important drawback is the semistructured nature of the storage of the time series data for each indicator. While a semistructured format is not in itself undesirable, the lack of a standard structure across indicators makes it difficult to automate operations to manipulate data in the database. Creating a new indicator derived from existing data in the Lotus Notes/Domino database would involve considerable skill and effort on the part of the QSCFA information technology staff. In practice, it would generally be much easier to download the data to, for example, a spreadsheet application, manipulate the data within the spreadsheet application, and then upload the resulting derived indicators to the database. However, this would defeat the goal of automating routine operations; as the source data are updated in the database, the information technology staff would have to repeat the download-manipulate-upload procedure for each derived indicator. This could be a constant burden as the source data are updated or corrected.

Based on these observations regarding the strengths and weaknesses of the existing prototype, we enumerated a series of recommendations in Chapter Four regarding the database architecture and database processing. These recommendations featured

- the establishment of standards for electronic data exchange with the Planning Council to eliminate manual data entry

- the use of a dedicated DBMS for data storage, manipulation, and retrieval

- the adoption of a three-tiered database architecture covering client, application server or Web server, and database server

- the implementation of the database user interface as a Web browser application using non-proprietary standards rather than a specific application

- the addition of provisions for ad hoc queries.

In addition, we also discussed the use of international coding and classification standards and recommended that, where appropriate, such classification numbers or codes be included in a searchable field of the database.

## Strategic Actions for Future Database Implementation

This analysis has identified a number of critical issues for meeting the short-term objectives of the QSCFA in terms of developing a social indicators database system. These issues pertain to the database objectives, the database architecture, the content of the database, and the database indicators. We conclude by recommending a number of strategic actions for the QSCFA to pursue in order to successfully implement the social indicators database system. Appendix B provides additional discussion of schedule and resource implications associated with the implementation of the database.

- *Develop a solid understanding of the various sources of data, their sample coverage, measures available, and strengths and limitations.* This project has made initial progress in this area, but it was not designed to be comprehensive in assessing the full range of possible data sources. This recommendation is particularly relevant for census and population-based surveys, which may be limited to coverage of specific populations (e.g., by nationality or age group) and where questions may deviate from international standards or vary over time. But similar issues may arise with respect to administrative sources of data or data from registries or vital statistics where there may have been important changes over time in how data were collected or recorded.

- *Conduct a complete review of data gaps for the preferred list of indicators.* With a solid understanding of the various sources of data and a prioritized list of indicators, it is possible to identify more clearly where gaps exist in the availability of the data needed to compute the desired list of indicators. Our assessment identified areas of likely gaps, but the project was not designed to definitively identify all gaps in the data. Among the gaps that stand out are those indicators that are typically available only through survey data and where survey data have not yet covered the relevant topics. For example, to our knowledge, there are no existing surveys that collect information on household debt or anthropometric measurements (e.g., height and weight) needed to assess obesity and other measures of nutritional status among children and adults. In addition to these obvious gaps, in some cases, data may exist to compute an indicator but a closer inspection of the quality of the data might suggest that the source of data has key limitations. In other cases, the data may be available but for only one point in time, and it might be desirable to update the information. Hence, a more preferred source of data should be sought.

- *Identify other indicators to examine in an in-depth review of measurement, data sources, and data quality.* We recommend that the QSCFA identify indicators that merit an in-depth review in terms of conceptual measurement, measurement given current data, and the consistency of measures over time and across data sources. We would suggest giving priority to key indicators across multiple departments, indicators that are complex to measure in theory and in practice, and measures that might derive from multiple data sources (e.g., different surveys or the same survey over time). Our list of priorities for indicators that would merit in-depth review would include the fertility rate; vital statistics on births and deaths and associated indicators derived from these data; measures of employment outcomes, such as the distribution of employment by class, occupation, and industry; measures of consumption, income, and poverty; education enrollment and attainment indicators; and health status and measures of health behaviors (e.g., smoking, drug use).

- *Determine whether some indicators must be recomputed to be consistent over time.* For certain key indicators, where it is known that changes in data processing or data sources over the years make an indicator less comparable over time, the QSCFA should consider accessing the original data to recompute the indictor using consistent methods over time. This means that the QSCFA database may not match the official, published value for a given indicator at any given point in time, but it would create a consistent indicator over time that can be used to assess progress.

- *Determine new data collection required.* Based on indicators that remain a priority but for which current data are not available or are not adequate, the QSCFA should assess the need for new data collection. In some cases, it may be possible to capture administrative data or data from registries in ways that have not been done before. In other cases, new data collection may be accomplished by revising or adding questions or modules to existing population-based surveys of families, households, or even businesses. For example, questions on household debt may be added to future waves of the HEIS. Likewise, health questions and anthropometric measurements could be added to future rounds of the FHS. New surveys may be designed as well. In such cases, consideration should be given to whether it is possible to collect data relevant for multiple indicators through a single, multipurpose survey rather than designing a series of special-purpose surveys.

- *Establish a formal mechanism for cooperation with the Planning Council in the implementation of the recommended database architecture.* The working relationship of the QSCFA and the Planning Council is vital to the successful implementation of the database of indicators. One of the principal recommendations regarding the database architecture is that standards be put in place for the electronic interchange of data between the Planning Council and the QSCFA. In addition, the QSCFA and the Planning Council should establish a mechanism for quality-assurance, maintenance, and updating of the source data for the indicators, as well as the appropriate methods to assure data confidentiality and security.

## Pursuing the Longer-Term Objectives

As noted above, we identified longer-term objectives for the QSCFA database, beyond a social indicators database system: namely, having the data and capacity to analyze relationships between variables and policy impacts. While the main focus in the near-term is on the social indicators database system, we recommended pursing this longer-term objective as well. In that regard, as a first step, the QSCFA can begin by developing the computing and staffing capacity needed to store and analyze the underlying microdata used to construct the social indicators (e.g., the various censuses, LFS, FHS, HEIS, and so on). This step would be relatively straightforward and is consistent with the discussion of the database architecture and database processing highlighted above.

A second step to pursue in parallel is the exploration of a new multipurpose survey focused on the specialized data needed to inform QSCFA decisions. In contrast to a single-purpose survey (e.g., a labor force survey), a multipurpose survey covers multiple topics in the same data source: economic data, demographic behaviors, health outcomes, human capital investments, and other aspects of family life.[2] When a multipurpose survey follows the same households and individuals over time, analyses are possible of the dynamics of decisionmaking within families: marriage and divorce, labor force entry and exit, schooling investments, changes in health status, responses to economic shocks (e.g., death of a household member), and so on. In developing such a survey, it will be critical to develop protocols to ensure the privacy of individuals and families for whom information is collected, including greater security provisions than what is required for a database of summary statistics. Such a multipurpose, longitudinal source of data does not currently exist in Qatar. Investing in such data, while admittedly a significant undertaking, would provide a rich source of information about the well-being of families, women, children, youth, the elderly, and those with special needs in Qatar's rapidly changing economic, cultural, and social environment. Ultimately, such data would permit a wealth of analyses of the relationships between outcomes and the impact of policy initiatives, and thereby strengthen the actions of the Council.

---

[2] There are a number of examples of such surveys implemented in various countries. Two such surveys include the Malaysian Family Life Surveys and the Indonesian Family Life Survey (see the RAND Corporation Labor and Population Program's overview of Family Life Surveys, online at http://www.rand.org/labor/FLS [as of March 18, 2006]).

# Appendix A: Proposed Database Architecture

In this appendix, we expand on our discussion of the technical recommendations for the database architecture we made in Chapter Four.

Based on our observations regarding the strengths and limitations of the existing prototype, we made the following recommendations:

- Establish standards for electronic data exchange.

- Use a DBMS for storage, manipulation, and retrieval of data.

- Adopt a three-tiered client/server database architecture: client, application server or Web server, and database server.

- Implement the database system user interface as a Web browser application using non-proprietary standards, rather than a Lotus Notes/Domino–specific application.

- Add a provision for ad hoc queries.

We discuss each of these in turn.

## Data Exchange Standards

As noted in Chapter Four, the vast majority of the indicators identified in this report are based on data published by the Planning Council. Such data are currently entered manually, which makes for a process that is laborious, time-consuming, and error-prone. Our first recommendation is that the QSCFA establish standards for electronic data exchange with the Planning Council and other agencies. In particular, we recommend adopting the non-proprietary XML standard for transmitting machine-readable databases, as XML is becoming the common representation language for document interchange over the Web. This would be in addition to any human-readable electronic provision of data by the Planning Council or other agencies (e.g., via Web pages.)

The QSCFA needs to have a standard for data transfer that is "machine-friendly," that is, a standard format that database and statistical software can readily export or import without much, if any, human intervention. Online access to data via a Web page or an Excel spreadsheet does not fulfill the requirement. Web pages are designed for the consumption of human beings; in general, it is quite difficult for machines to extract data from Web pages in an automated way, even those Web pages that consist primarily of tables. Similarly, Excel spreadsheet tables are designed for human beings, not machines, to read and analyze. Creating a program to import data from many different Excel spreadsheets into the QSCFA indicators database would be quite difficult, as the program potentially must have a different procedure to handle each individual table. It would generally be much faster and easier (though laborious, tedious, and error-prone) for a human being to "cut and paste" data from a spreadsheet into the database.

The standard could be either proprietary or non-proprietary. Proprietary standards are those based on a software package that is owned and under the control of an individual or firm. Proprietary standards for data files include the native formats for commercial database and statistical packages, such as Oracle®, SAS®, or SPSS®. Non-proprietary standards include flat ASCII files and XML, a standard in wide use for Web-based data systems.

Proprietary standards should typically be avoided. Adopting a proprietary standard would potentially lock the QSCFA in to a particular vendor or software package, making it difficult to migrate the data to a newer and better system at a later date. Supporting agencies may find it difficult to support the proprietary format if they do not use the associated software.

For this reason, we recommend that the QSCFA adopt the non-proprietary XML as the standard format for data exchange. XML is closely related to HTML, used in Web pages. XML has been widely adopted as the standard format for data exchange on the Internet. XML also has the advantage of being human-readable, unlike most proprietary formats. This particular standard is supported by all major database software, and many major statistical software packages. Figures A.1 and A.2 show an example of a dataset and the corresponding XML code.

It is important to note that XML, alone, does not specify how data elements that appear in an XML document should be interpreted. For example, the element "3.14159" could be interpreted as either a floating-point number or as a string. XML also, by itself, does not specify a particular data structure, i.e., it does not specify what fields and elements are expected to be in a dataset. Thus, we recommend that one of the XML schema languages, such as RELAX NG (Regular Language Description for XML) or World Wide Web Consortium (W3C) XML Schema, be used in conjunction with XML. These languages are used to describe the data structure for an XML file, and a schema specification written in these languages can be used to automate checking that an XML file holds the correct types and numbers of data elements, as well as specifying how individual data elements are to be interpreted.

| Population | Year | Age | Sex | Nationality | Count |
|---|---|---|---|---|---|
| | 2003 | 0 | Male | Qatar | 3100 |
| | 2003 | 1 | Male | Qatar | 12300 |
| | 2003 | 5 | Male | Qatar | 13100 |

Figure A.1—The First Three Observations in the "Population" Data Set Giving Population Counts by Year, Age, Sex, and Nationality

```
<?xml version="1.0" standalone="yes">

<Population>
        <Observation>
                <Year>2003</Year>
                <Age>0</Age>
                <Sex>Male</Sex>
                <Nationality>Qatar</Nationality>
                <Count>3100</Count>
        </Observation>
        <Observation>
                <Year>2003</Year>
                <Age>1</Age>
                <Sex>Male</Sex>
                <Nationality>Qatar</Nationality>
                <Count>12300</Count>
        </Observation>
        <Observation>
                <Year>2003</Year>
                <Age>5</Age>
                <Sex>Male</Sex>
                <Nationality>Qatar</Nationality>
                <Count>13100</Count>
        </Observation>
        ...
</ Population>
```

Figure A.2—First Three Observations of the "Population" Dataset in XML Format

# Database Management System

As discussed in Chapter Four, three of the limitations of the prototype database are largely due to the limitations of the software platform used to implement the prototype. While the characteristics of the native database of Lotus Notes/Domino make it a useful platform for creating prototype applications to demonstrate capabilities, these characteristics can lead to difficulty in a production environment. Thus, our second recommendation is to adopt a dedicated DBMS for storage and manipulation of data.

Below, we discuss two alternative database systems, the RDBMS and a DBMS designed to support data warehouses.

## Relational Database Management System

The relational model provides a good match to the type of data that would be stored in the QSCFA social indicators database system. Each indicator in the database can be thought of as a table. Some of the indicators, such as per capita GDP, could be represented as a table with a single column and a row for each year. Others, such as population count, could be represented by a table with multiple columns (such as year, age, gender, and nationality), and have a row corresponding to each unique combination of year, age, gender, and so on.

In technical terms, each indicator would be a *relation* (or table) in a *relational database.* Each relation would have a set of *attributes*, which includes the year of the data, and an attribute for each of the subgroups of interest. In the "Population" example in Table A.1, the attributes are Year, Age, Sex, Nationality, and Count. Each of the attributes would have an associated *domain*, or set of valid values.[1] For example, the attribute Sex could have the domain {Male, Female}. Further examples of the domains that may be associated with each of the attributes in the "Population" database are given in Table A.1. Each observation in the relation will have a *key*, a set of attributes that uniquely describes the observation. In the "Population" example in Table A.1, the key is {Year, Age, Sex, Nationality}.

Modern relational databases also provide a standard language, SQL, which can be used to retrieve and manipulate the data. SQL queries could be made against

---

[1] Note that here the term *domain* is being used in a different sense from how it was used earlier in this report, where it was used to refer to the subject domain of an indicator. Here, it is used in the mathematical sense, in which the term domain refers to the set of values a particular variable may take.

**Table A.1—Informal Definition and Example Domains for Each Attribute in the Population Relation**

| Attribute | Meaning | Domain |
|---|---|---|
| Year | Year of observation | 1970, 1971, 1972, ..., 2002, 2003, 2004 |
| Age | First year of age group. The first age group is 0 years, the second is 1–4 years, the third is 5–9 years, and five-year age intervals thereafter. The final, open-ended interval is 85+ | 0, 1, 5, 10, 15, 20, 25, 30, 35, 40, 45, 50, 55, 60, 65, 70, 75, 80, 85 |
| Sex | The gender | Male, Female |
| Nationality | The nationality, Qatari or non-Qatari | Qatar, Other |
| Count | The population count for a particular combination of year, age, sex, and nationality | Non-negative integers (0, 1, 2, ...) |

the "Population" relation to yield total population by year; by age, sex and nationality; or, indeed, by any subset of the key attributes. For example, the SQL query

```
SELECT      SUM(Count)
FROM        PopulationByYearAgeSexNationality
GROUP BY    Year, Sex
```

would retrieve the "Population" relation and compute the total population of Qatar by year and gender. Another SQL query would compute the total population of Qatar by year and nationality:

```
SELECT      SUM(Count)
FROM        PopulationByYearAgeSexNationality
GROUP BY    Year, Nationality
```

Thus, one base table could serve to produce multiple measures.

## Data Warehouse

A data warehouse is a database designed specifically to support rapid online analysis of large amounts of data. It is optimized for online analysis and reports. A data warehouse is generally implemented as part of a larger system that takes source data from many databases, transforms the data into a form optimized for analysis, loads it into the data warehouse, and provides online analytical processing (OLAP) or executive information system (EIS) tools for working with the database.

A data warehouse differs from more general database management systems in several ways. It is oriented toward large, infrequently updated datasets, where many users require only read-only access and where the typical query involves large numbers of individual records. In contrast, a general DBMS is designed to correctly implement online transaction processing (OLTP). In OLTP, the database is updated frequently by many users who require both read- and write-access, and the typical query involves a few individual records. A general DBMS will keep track of who is updating what record to ensure that conflicting updates or requests do not occur. A data warehouse can be faster at retrieving and processing large amounts of data than a general DBMS because it can avoid the overhead associated with ensuring the correct implementation of OLTP.

A data warehouse database can also offer improved performance over a more general DBMS database by precomputing and storing the results of possible queries. This can include merging datasets together, performing cross-tabulations at all possible levels of aggregation, storing the results of frequently required formulas, and so on. The increased response speed for queries comes at the expense of storage space; data warehouse databases that store all the results of all possible queries will be considerably larger than the source databases. In practice, the designers of a data warehouse may make an assessment of the queries that are most likely to be made, and precompute and store only the corresponding responses; this results in a smaller storage space requirement but inferior performance for "unlikely" queries.

## Three-Tier System Architecture

As discussed in Chapter Four, the third recommendation is to adopt a three-tiered client/server architecture to support the use of either a RDBMS or a data warehouse system, and to provide more flexibility and functionality for end users. The three tiers consist of (1) a client tier, which provides a GUI or Web browser; (2) an application server or Web server tier, which provides application programs or Web pages to act as intermediaries between the client and the database server, and can provide for access-control and other security measures; and (3) a database server tier, which provides the database management system. This architecture is widely used in Web applications, particularly in e-commerce.

The three-tier architecture is a result of the natural evolution of computing systems over the decades. Until the 1970s, data systems were typically one-tiered, with all database, application, and user-interface functions residing on one machine, typically a mainframe computer accessed by users using "dumb terminals." As personal computers became more widely available in the 1980s, systems moved toward a client-server architecture, where the database and application tiers would typically reside on a server (either a mainframe, mini, or personal computer), and the user interface (and perhaps some of the application logic) would reside on a client machine, a personal computer, or "smart terminal." In the 1990s, with the advent of the World Wide Web and wider public access to the Internet, the three-tier architecture came into use, particularly for e-commerce applications. The three tiers consist of a database server, an application server to generate dynamic Web pages along with a static Web page server, and a Web browser. The Web server tier acts as an intermediary between the Web client software and the database system software, translating user input from the Web browser into database queries, and reformatting and translating the response of the database server into a form suitable for Web browsers.

The current prototype uses a two-tier architecture, with Lotus Domino serving as both the database and application server, and Lotus Notes as the client. The tight integration of the database and application tiers can be useful, but it also makes the prototype database highly dependent on the underlying software architecture of Lotus Notes/Domino and the internal implementation details of the database. This would make it difficult to migrate the database system to other software packages or platforms. It also limits the ability of the database to interface with other database systems that do not use the Lotus Notes/Domino software.

By way of contrast, the three-tier architecture is easier to maintain and update, and can be designed to insulate the end user from details of the physical setup of the database. It is flexible enough to allow for multiple, distributed database servers that may reside in different physical locations, e.g., the QSCFA and the Planning Council. It does this by dividing the database system into components, where each component communicates using standard interfaces. The interfaces are designed so that the data are specified in a way that is not dependent on the physical location of the data on some storage device, or the implementation details of the database management system software.

This architecture could be implemented in several different ways, using different software for each of the three tiers. For example, the database tier could be implemented in any one of a number of DBMSs, such as Oracle® RDBMS or IBM® DB2®; the application tier in Apache/Perl (Practical Extraction and Report Language)/PHP (hypertext preprocessor)/Python or Lotus Domino, or any one of a number of Java-based application servers,[2] and the client tier in Lotus Notes or a Web browser. One application stack in wide use is LAMP, which is an acronym for the components Linux, Apache, MySQL, and Perl/PHP/Python. It is popular in part because each of the individual components is free software available under the GNU Public License. One alternative that deserves serious consideration is one of the data warehouse OLAP systems. There are a plethora of choices available.

## Web-Based Implementation

The fourth recommendation provided in Chapter Four is to implement the indicators database as a Web-based system using non-proprietary standards, rather than a Lotus Notes/Domino–specific application. This recommendation stems from two factors. If the indicators database system is Web-based, it will ease integration with other Web-based resources. A Web-based system using non-proprietary standards will free the database from dependence upon any particular software manufacturer. This will aid in ensuring that the database can be migrated to newer and better environments as the state of the art improves. The ease of integration with other Web-based resources is useful, in particular because of the stated intention of the Planning Council to provide a Web-based interface for the QSCFA indicators that they are tasked with producing. Such an interface may also be possible in the future for other government ministries and other external sources of data for the social indicators database system.

By "Web-based" we do not mean simply that the system is accessible via the World Wide Web. Instead, we mean that the system itself is built to take advantage of the various non-proprietary standards for information exchange that have developed along with the Web. Chief among these standards is XML, but there are also other standards worth considering, such as SOAP (Simple Object Access Protocol) for exchanging XML-based messages using HTTP over a computer network. Most of these standards are promulgated by the World Wide Web Consortium.[3]

It is desirable that any standards used for data exchange be both open and non-proprietary. By open we mean that the standard is published and is easily accessible. Note that some open standards require licensing fees for implementation. By non-proprietary we mean that the standard is not owned by any particular individual. The XML standard is both open and non-proprietary.

---

[2] Java™ is a registered trademark of Sun Microsystems, Inc.

[3] The World Wide Web Consortium is online at http://www.w3c.org (as of March 18, 2006).

By using open, non-proprietary standards in implementing the database system, the QSCFA can avoid being "trapped" by a particular vendor and can take advantage of new technologies as they come along.

Having a Web-based system will also facilitate integration with other data systems that make data available on the Web or that are themselves Web-based. Integration can be as simple as providing a link to the appropriate Web page. At the opposite end of the spectrum, such a Web-based system could serve as the foundation for a nationwide distributed database system for social statistics.

## Ad Hoc Queries

Our fifth recommendation, detailed in Chapter Four, is to add a provision for ad hoc queries. The recommended list of indicators provided in Chapter Three is our best assessment of the set of indicators that are currently needed by the QSCFA to execute its missions. However, the needs of the QSCFA may change over time, or new data or ways of looking at data may come to light. Thus, we recommend that in addition to providing the listed indicators, the system provide some mechanism for ad hoc queries. This will help to ensure that the database system will continue to be relevant into the future.

This type of capability is build into OLAP systems. It is also provided as add-on software by many database software vendors. In addition to providing the ability to perform basic cross-tabulations ("pivots"), such software often provides the capability to do more advanced operations, such as regression analysis.

The ability to perform ad hoc queries is dependent on having access to base data at an appropriate level of disaggregation to support the ad hoc queries. If only the derived tables of indicators originally specified are available in the database, ad hoc queries would be limited in scope. If, however, base data are available at the individual or family level, ad hoc queries could potentially support nearly any desired measure.

One issue of note is that ad hoc queries, in conjunction with access to individual- or family-level data, could lead to compromising individual privacy unless suitable security measures are implemented. These measures could include deleting selected data fields on individual or family records to render identifying unique individuals or families infeasible, or "statistical security" software features that prevent successive queries on overlapping subsets of observations that could be used to identify a specific individual. In any case, due care must be taken with security in order to prevent abuse and violation of privacy.

# Appendix B: Organization, Resource, and Timeline Considerations

In this appendix, we discuss various considerations associated with implementing the recommendations in this report to create a social indicators database system for the QSCFA. The considerations associated with this project include:

- *Organizational issues:* how to locate the activity within the organizational structure of the QSCFA

- *Resource requirements:* the project manpower requirements, activities to outsource, the hardware and software requirements, and implications for QSCFA staff training and development

- *Timeline:* the timetable for project implementation.

This discussion, which addresses each of these issues in turn, is intended to serve as a useful starting point for the QSCFA to develop an implementation plan for the social indicators database system project. As such, we note four caveats.

First, the approaches we discuss here are meant to be a guide to aid the QSCFA in planning and execution, rather than a definitive roadmap. The approach we offer and the resource and time requirements we estimate are based on our professional judgment from our personal experience with similar efforts at RAND and other institutions. It is to be expected that our estimates may differ from those of information technology personnel and other staff more deeply familiar with the capabilities of the QSCFA and other institutions within Qatar.

While the recommendations we make here may not accord with the final approach, they can provide a useful vehicle for discussion and interaction, and serve as the starting point for developing a more refined plan as revisions are proposed, debated, and incorporated. Thus, to be successful, our recommendations must be modified by the considered judgment of the information technology professionals, statisticians, social scientists, and domain area experts implementing the project at the QSCFA. Our suggested approach and resource and time estimates must initially be reviewed in light of the final objective of the project: an information system to support the goals and fundamental missions of the QSCFA. After this initial review and after an implementation plan is adopted, we recommend that the QSCFA regularly review and revise the plan to see that it is clearly leading in a direction that will meet the final objective.

Second, in the course of implementing the project, new information will come to light that will call for revisions of planned approaches to organization, resources, and the timeline. This is natural and to be expected; developing complex systems calls for frequent assessment of lessons learned about how difficult or easy it is to implement features of the system. The process also calls for frequent interaction and feedback from the end users as to the utility and appropriateness of the features of the system. Thus, consistent with the first point, some flexibility in the implementation of the project is desirable so that the new information that is acquired in the development process can be incorporated to improve the end result.

Third, in the discussion that follows, our primary focus is on the approach and requirements needed to meet the short-term objectives of the social indicators database system as discussed in Chapter Two. Namely, the short-term goal is to develop a social indicators database system to help QSCFA staff and senior decisionmakers make appropriate policy decisions. Thus, the immediate tasks are those associated with developing the database architecture and populating the database with the desired social indicators. However, as noted in Chapter Two, decisionmaking at the QSCFA would be enhanced by pursing a longer-term goal of establishing a database containing data more suited to assessing the relationships between indicators (including cause-and-effect relationships) and the effects of specific policies. While our main focus in this appendix is the approach and requirements for meeting the short-term objective, our approach also takes into consideration the needs required to support the long-term objective as well. This means that some choices in the design of the database architecture will be made that may not be strictly necessary in order to support the short-term goal, but that will make the attainment of the long-term goal much easier.

Fourth, the recommendations made in this report regarding the architecture of the social indicators database system leaves scope for several different implementation approaches. We can classify the approaches into three different general strategies. One strategy involves a minimalist approach wherein the QSCFA would continue to use Lotus Notes/Domino as the front end to the system, while upgrading the back end of the system with a relational database. A second strategy would be to use a relational database as the back end to a Web application server, from which users would access the data using their Web browsers. The third strategy is a variant of the second: the relational database is used to store the source databases, a data warehouse is used to store a working dataset, and Online Analytical Processing tools are used (via the Web) to access the data.

The different approaches have different implications for the cost of the system, the maintainability of the system, and the ease of integrating features that would support the long-term goal of allowing the QSCFA to work with individual- and family-level data. The discussion that follows does not presume which strategy is adopted by the QSCFA. Instead, our recommendations are designed to be relevant for any of these approaches. However, it does mean that some finer details of project implementation and resource requirements would need to be developed depending upon which approach is taken.

## Organization

The database of social indications will serve multiple constituencies within the QSCFA, as discussed in Chapter Two. This includes the various departments focused on the family, women, children, youth, the elderly, and people with special needs, as well as staff involved in research and analysis. In addition, the Information Technology Department is essential for providing relevant technical expertise and support. The organization within the QSCFA of the project to implement the database should thus recognize this diverse group of stakeholders.

Currently, the prototype database project is housed within the Information Technology Department, which is appropriate given the heavy emphasis to date on developing the software to support the prototype database. For the next phase of the project, our recommendation is to house the project within the Statistics and Analysis Department, as shown in the organization chart in Figure B.1. In addition, we recommend that the project be guided by an Advisory Committee that is chaired by the head of the Statistics and Analysis Department. The committee members would consist of at least one staff member from each of the other relevant departments, including Information Technology, as well as the six domain area departments. (In Figure B.1, the Advisory Committee is shown in a dashed box to indicate the cross-departmental nature of the committee.) This advisory committee would ideally meet at least quarterly to review the implementation plan, discuss issues that have arisen since the last meeting, and make any needed adjustments to the implementation plan. (The specific staffing of the project is discussed below.)

116

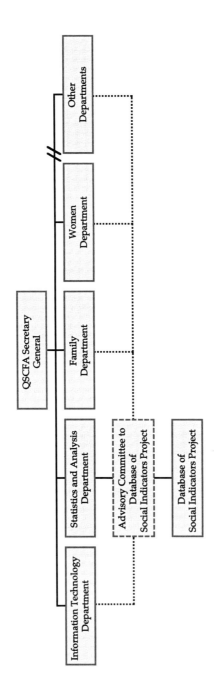

Figure B.1—Organizational Chart for Database Project

This organizational structure recognizes that the further development of the database must draw on the technical expertise of the Information Technology Department and the methodological expertise of the Statistics and Analysis Department, as well as the substantive expertise of the six domain area departments. Each constituency will participate on the Advisory Committee, while the overall responsibility for the project will reside with the Statistics and Analysis Department. This is appropriate given the ultimate objective of the database to serve decisionmaking within the QSCFA.

Once the database is developed and operational, this organizational structure can continue to serve the ongoing needs of the QSCFA with respect to the social indicators database system. For example, we recommended that the indicators in the database be reviewed at least annually, with decisions made about indicators to add or delete, and how historical information should be maintained. These are all issues that can be decided within the structure of the Advisory Committee. By representing the user community, the Committee will have the best perspective to help recommend improvements over time.

## Resources

The resource requirements can be segmented into the personnel required to staff the project, the activities to outsource to external vendors, the hardware and software requirements, and the needs for staff training and development. We discuss each of these aspects in turn.

### *Project Staffing*

The personnel requirements to carry out the tasks associated with developing the database and subsequently maintaining the database and associated software programs is subject to some uncertainty because it will depend on the implementation details of the database. We can, however, outline the roles that will need to be performed by staff with some confidence and suggest possible staffing based on the functions that need to be performed.

The functions fall into four areas:

1.  *Project leadership.* The project leader will have overall responsibility for construction and maintenance of the database. He or she will supervise the other staff associated with the project, and will also supervise any contractor staff. Consistent with the organizational structure discussed

above, this individual will report to the head of the Statistics and Analysis Department and will staff the project Advisory Committee.

2. *Database administration.* One staff member will be the database administrator. The database administrator is expected to be familiar with the database software used to implement the proof-of-concept and operational versions of the database. The database administrator is charged with dealing with all technical details associated with populating and maintaining the database of indicators.

3. *Systems programming.* One staff member will be the systems programmer. The systems programmer is to have the primary responsibility for matters dealing with system integration, that is, for those matters that pertain to linking the database tier with the application and presentation tiers of the database system. He or she will also take the lead on software and possible hardware issues dealing with online links to the supporting agencies that provide the data to the QSCFA.

4. *Applications programming.* The applications programmer will be charged with maintaining and updating the application tier of the architecture. He or she will need to be familiar with the system that stands between the user and the database.

One possible staffing configuration is to assign a single person to each role. In this case, there will be four staff: a project leader, database administrator, systems programmer, and applications programmer; the latter three report to the project leader. This configuration is shown in the project staff organization chart in Figure B.2.

It may be feasible, especially during the initial phase of creation of the database of indicators, to combine roles. One configuration, for example, would combine the roles of project leader and database administrator. This would result in a reduction in the overall staffing level of the project by one person. There are limits, however, to the staff reduction that can occur by combining roles; it is extremely unlikely, for example, that one would be able to locate an individual who could successfully take on all four roles at once.

Beyond these staff requirements, one of the challenges associated with this project will be the uncertainty associated with obtaining and working with the necessary data. Many of the problems in combining data for a given year or in making data comparable across time may only come to light when working with the actual data. Thus, there is a great deal of uncertainty associated with the level

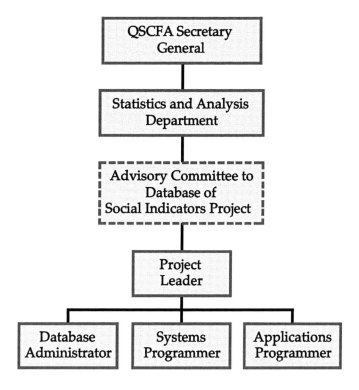

Figure B.2—Organizational Chart for Database Project Staff

of effort required to make an operational database of indicators. These staff may be drawn from existing staff, for example, from the Statistics and Analysis Department. Alternatively, new staff may be added to focus on the strategic activities identified in our recommendations: developing an understanding of the various sources of data, reviewing data gaps for the preferred list of indicators; conducting an in-depth review of other key indicators, determining whether some indicators need to be recomputed, and giving consideration to new data collection required. Alternatively, some or all of these activities could be outsourced, as we note below.

## Data Transfer

We anticipate that the new database system will be mainly populated with data from machine-readable sources provided by supporting agencies such as the Planning Council. However, the current prototype database system contains data elements (e.g., Human Development Indicators, international statutes) that will not be provided by supporting agencies in machine-readable form. Thus, these data will have to be transferred to the new database system from the existing prototype database system.

We have already noted that the structure of the data in the prototype database renders it difficult and time-consuming to automate data manipulation. Thus, we recommend that the data transfer task be done manually, using a cut-and-paste procedure to transfer the data to the new database system. Given the small number of measures that fall into this category, we estimate that on the order of one person-week would be required to execute this task. Because this task will not be automated, we further recommend that some set quality-control procedure be followed to ensure that the data transfer task has been executed correctly.

## *Outsourcing*

Implementing any database can be a potentially complex, time-consuming, and costly activity. The QSCFA database combines data from a wide variety of sources, contributing to the complexity. In addition, there are a number of implementation choices that will have to be made; chief among them is the decision to store just the pre-calculated indicators specified in this document, or (as we recommend) to store the source datasets used to generate the indicators and to dynamically generate the indicators in addition to storing the pre-calculated (and in many cases, officially published) indicators.

The scale and complexity of this project is such that we anticipate that the database should not be built in-house, but instead should be outsourced to a vendor. Outsourcing the initial construction of the database will allow QSCFA to more easily explore alternative methods for implementing the database through soliciting vendor proposals as to the appropriate means for implementation. In addition, outsourcing will eliminate the need to permanently staff the QSCFA with expertise that may only be needed during the start-up phase. Thus, the timetable we outline below assumes that the initial database system will be created by an outside vendor.

Moreover, as we discuss further below, the uncertainties associated with the database development lead us to recommend a two-phase approach: first, the development of a proof-of-concept system, and second, the development of a production system. The development of the proof-of-concept system will allow both the QSCFA and the software vendor to gather information as to the uncertainties associated with developing the system. This will allow both to be better informed when it comes time to write the contract for the final production system; both will have a better understanding as to the relative ease or difficulty of implementing different aspects of the database system, and thus can enter into the contract with less uncertainty.

Beyond the development of the database software, other activities associated with the project may be outsourced as well. This includes the set of activities identified in the set of recommendations as strategic actions for future implementation of the database. These include developing an understanding of the various sources of data, reviewing data gaps for the preferred list of indicators, conducting an in-depth review of other key indicators, determining whether some indicators need to be recomputed, and giving consideration to new data collection required.

## Hardware and Software Requirements

The precise hardware and software requirements will, naturally, be dependent upon the choice among the three general implementation strategies noted at the outset of this appendix. In terms of hardware, either one or two server-class machines will be required for all three tiers of the database, along with mass storage to hold the database and any derived data. One possible set-up is to have one dedicated server solely for the database server and a second dedicated server for the application and presentation tiers.

The storage space requirements for the indicators database are going to be implementation-dependent. If the QSCFA decides to go the route of using only aggregated data, then the storage requirements are likely to be quite small. We estimate that each year of data should take no more than one megabyte of storage space. One gigabyte of storage space would hold data for all available years with room to spare. The relatively small size is due to the relatively high level of aggregation anticipated for the indicators. Even for a measure broken down for each combination of subgroups (e.g., gender, age, nationality, special needs, headship, and geographic location), this would only result in up to 20,000 discrete numbers per year. It is likely that the metadata (surveys, manuals, spreadsheets, and the like) that document the data will take up more storage space than the data itself.

If, however, the QSCFA decides to go the route of implementing the indicators database as a data warehouse, the storage requirements would grow considerably as the QSCFA would need to store all the source datasets as well as the data "cubes" that serve as the basis of the data warehouse. In this case, we estimate that the data for all available years would take a few tens of gigabytes (at most) for data storage, and up to a terabyte for the full data warehouse. Given that the current price for a terabyte of disk storage is well under 10,0000 Qatari Riyals, this is no cause for concern.

The software required will also be implementation-dependent. One thing we can anticipate is that there will be separate software modules for the database tier, the application tier, and the presentation tier. The cost of software to implement a database system such as the indicators database can vary widely. For example, the LAMP consists of several software components, each of which is free: the Linux operating system, the Apache Web server, the MySQL relational database, and the Perl, Python, and PHP scripting languages. LAMP is a popular application stack for designing data-driven Web applications. Non-free alternatives can run from the tens to hundreds of thousands of Qatari Riyals; proprietary systems are available from IBM, Oracle, and many other vendors.

It is important to bear in mind during the procurement process that the cost of software is a relatively small component of the total lifecycle cost of a system. The initial cost associated with software tends to be overwhelmed by the costs associated with customizing and maintaining a system to suit the needs of the users. In the case of the QSCFA, the primary drivers of lifecycle cost are likely to be the labor associated with obtaining, cleaning, recoding and loading data into the system. To the extent that it is feasible, the QSCFA should offload these tasks to the supporting agencies. Another major driver of lifecycle cost will be customizing the output to suit the needs of the user; this is one reason why an ability to perform ad hoc queries is highly desirable, as it will allow the sophisticated user or the applications programmer to easily fill this need.

## Staff Training and Development

A final resource requirement concerns the need to provide training and other support for the QSCFA staff who will be users of the database. Depending upon the implementation approach, especially the user interface that is developed, such training may be more modest or more extensive. Our recommendation is that a small group of initial users be employed from the early stages of the project to serve as test users of the new system so that the training requirements can be readily identified. One natural approach would be to use staff on the Advisory Committee in this role. The group of early users or "beta-testers" can make recommendations for any written documentation that may be required, as well as the structure of any in-house training courses. They will develop sufficient expertise with the database that they can also become an ongoing resource for staff who are new users of the system.

# Timeline

Taking into account the requirements for meeting the short-term and long-term objectives of the database project, our assessment is that the QSCFA could attain the following milestones over a three-year time horizon:

1. Have a fully operational database of indicators that is routinely used by QSCFA staff in evaluating current programs, in proposing changes to current programs, and in proposing new policies and programs. In so far as it is possible, the database would contain indicators that are defined consistently over time, so that year-to-year comparisons can be made and data-updating operations in the database would be automated, with source agencies providing electronic files containing the information needed to populate the database, and with database software to take the data files and update the database as appropriate.

2. Be well on the way to having the necessary databases and tools to do in-depth analyses that identify the pathways of causation for those issues of key interest to the QSCFA. The database would contain many of the key sources of social, demographic, and economic data—the censuses, vital statistics, labor force surveys, health surveys, and so on—so they are readily available to the QSCFA staff for analysis. The QSCFA would also have the necessary expertise available in-house so that statisticians and other analysts can perform the appropriate tasks—exploratory data analysis, multivariate regression analysis, and so on—needed to support domain experts in their search for problems and solutions. Additional efforts needed to gather data on pressing issues—new surveys, for example—would be well under way.

In presenting a more detailed timetable in this section, we focus on those activities that could be accomplished over the initial 12 months of the project.

Figure B.3 presents a detailed timeline associated with the tasks required to develop the social indicators database system. Given the uncertainties associated with the project, we recommend a two-stage approach. In the first stage of development, the "proof-of-concept" stage, a fully capable version of the database will be developed for a carefully selected subset of the indicators. We suggest that this subset of indicators draw from each of the key datasets that will be used to generate the full set of indicators: the censuses, vital statistics data, administrative data (e.g., data from the Ministries of Health and Education), survey data (e.g., data from the LFS or HEIS), and so on. The subset of indicators should include the indicators examined in depth in this report and otherwise drawn from those indicators given a priority ranking (a ranking of 1, or possibly 2, in Table 3.3 in Chapter Three). It should also include population counts, which are used to calculate the ratios reported for many indicators. In the second stage, a fully operational production version of the database will be developed and populated with the full set of indicators.

Restricting the proof-of-concept system to a subset of indicators has the virtue of limiting the uncertainty faced by both the QSCFA and any potential bidder for this project. This will reduce the amount of the "risk premium" that might be added to the amount bid for the project. It will also increase the chance of success and make potential bidders more likely to enter a bid for the project.

The schedule shown in Figure B.3 explicitly allocates time for gathering the test and operational datasets needed to create the proof-of-concept system and initial operational database. In each case, the time allocated to gathering the data occurs before actual development. This is done to ensure that costly delays due to a lack of data do not occur during the actual development cycle. Of course, during the development process the QSCFA may discover that additional data are needed, or that a different format for the source datasets is desirable. Thus, the QSCFA may need to obtain additional data or reformat the source datasets during the process of development. However, ensuring that at least the majority of data are available prior to the initiation of development will help to avoid interruptions in the development process, as work can carry forward on elements of the database with finalized data while the QSCFA works to resolve any problems that come to light with the remainder of the data.

As seen in Figure B.3, the entire process for creating the database of indicators—from developing a proof-of-concept system to building an initial operational version—is envisioned to take one year. The figure assumes a start date of January 2006. The schedule can easily be adapted to any start date by shifting the schedule either earlier or later.

125

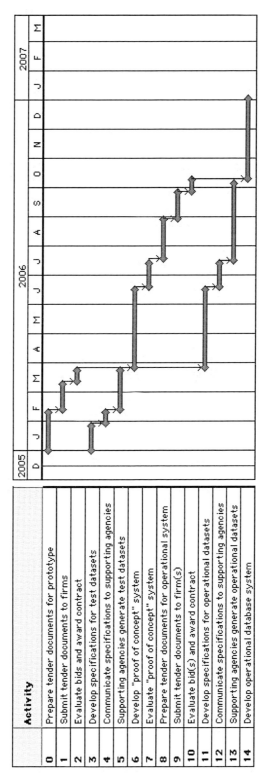

Figure B.3—Proposed Schedule for Project Implementation

# Bibliography

Al-Jaber, Khalifa A., and Samir M. Farid, *Qatar Family Health Survey 1998: Principal Report*, Doha, Qatar: Ministry of Health, 2000.

Economic and Social Commission for Western Asia, World Summit on the Information Society, "Partnership List of ICT Indicators," background material for Capacity-Building Workshop on Information Society Measurements: Core Indicators, Statistics, and Data Collection, Beirut, June 7–10, 2005. Online at http://www.escwa.org.lb/wsis/meetings/7-10june/0B1aPartnershipListofICTIndicatorsESCWA.pdf (as of March 17, 2006).

ESCWA—see Economic and Social Commission for Western Asia.

Lerman, Robert, and Shlomo Yitzhaki, "A Note on the Calculation and Interpretation of the Gini Index," *Economic Letters*, Vol. 15, No. 3–4, 1984, pp. 363–368.

Qatar Planning Council, *Sample Labour Force Survey, April 2001*, Doha, Qatar: State of Qatar Planning Council, April 2002.

———, *Annual Statistical Abstract*, Doha, Qatar: State of Qatar Planning Council, 23rd Issue, 2003.

———, *Annual Statistical Abstract*, Doha, Qatar: State of Qatar Planning Council, 24th Issue, 2004.

———, "Summary of Qatar Census 2004: Population," Doha, Qatar: State of Qatar Planning Council, 2005a. Online at http://www.planning.gov.qa/Census_2004/population/index_e.htm (as of March 18, 2006).

———, *Vital Statistics Annual Bulletin Marriages and Divorces*, Doha, Qatar: State of Qatar Planning Council, 21st Issue, June 2005b. Online at http://www.planning.gov.qa/other_publications/Marriages_Divorces2005.pdf (as of March 18, 2006).

Qatar Supreme Council for Family Affairs, *The Supreme Council for Family Affairs*, Doha, Qatar: State of Qatar Supreme Council for Family Affairs, undated brochure.

———, *The Elderly in the State of Qatar*, Doha, Qatar: State of Qatar Supreme Council for Family Affairs, 2002.

———, *Women and Men in Qatar: Statistical View 2004*, Doha, Qatar: State of Qatar Supreme Council for Family Affairs, 2004.

QSCFA—see Qatar Supreme Council for Family Affairs.

128

Thomas, Scott L., and Amy E. Peasley, *Lotus Notes Certification: Application Development and System Administration*, New York: McGraw-Hill, 1998.

UNDP—see United Nations Development Programme.

United Nations Development Programme, *Human Development Report 2003*, New York: Oxford University Press, 2003. Online at http://hdr.undp.org/reports/global/2003/ (as of March 18, 2006).

———, *Human Development Report 2004*, New York: United Nations Development Programme, 2004. Online at http://hdr.undp.org/reports/global/2004/?CFID=318490&CFTOKEN=91993609 (as of March 18, 2006).

United Nations Statistics Division, *1993 System of National Accounts*, Brussels/Luxembourg, New York, Paris, and Washington, D.C.: Commission of the European Communities, International Monetary Fund, Organisation for Economic Co-operation and Development, United Nations, and World Bank, 1993. Online at http://unstats.un.org/unsd/sna1993/toctop.asp (as of March 17, 2006).

———, "ISIC Rev.3.1: Detailed Structure and Explanatory Notes," *International Standard Industrial Classification of All Economic Activities, Revision 3.1*, March 2002. Online at http://unstats.un.org/unsd/cr/registry/regcst.asp?Cl=17 (as of March 17, 2006).